Formerly a Partner and Head of Intellectual Property at Osborne Clarke in London with over 25 year' experience of advising on intellectual property in all its forms, Lorna is now a Consultant to the firm. She is the author and co-author of several books in the field and regularly lectures on intellectual property at a range of conferences in Europe and around the world.

Protecting Unregistered Brands: A Practical Guide to the Law of Passing Off

Protecting Unregistered Brands: A Practical Guide to the Law of Passing Off

Lorna Brazell
BSc (Hons), LLM, Solicitor-Advocate

Law Brief Publishing

Published 2020 by Law Brief Publishing, an imprint of Law Brief Publishing Ltd
30 The Parks
Minehead
Somerset
TA24 8BT

www.lawbriefpublishing.com

Paperback: 978-1-912687-77-0

PREFACE

The law of passing off originates in decisions of the English courts in the nineteenth century and, as a creature purely of the common law, has been evolving through further case law ever since.

In the twenty first century, its evolution has hastened as globalisation has brought into conflict companies which formerly had no contact with either each other or each other's customers, and as the internet has introduced new ways of doing business and interacting with potential customers. This evolution is bound to continue as the online world continues to grow in commercial importance, and the issues to which marketing through social media channels, within online virtual worlds or multiplayer games are giving rise are brought before the courts. Consequently, the state of the law as set out in this book, at 31 January 2020, will soon be revised further as cases addressing these issues come to be decided. Nevertheless, the principles on which the tort is based remain those which the courts of previous centuries laid down, and future decisions must be assessed based on these. This brief introduction aims to set out the principles and the thinking behind the leading cases in a way which will help those trying to apply them to new situations identify where and how the tort can be invoked.

Lorna Brazell
January 2020

CONTENTS

CHAPTER ONE
INTRODUCTION: WHEN AND WHY DO WE NEED A TORT OF PASSING OFF?

Overview

The common law tort of passing off is one of the small group of economic torts. It is generally treated as a branch of the law of intellectual property but, within that category, is something of an outsider. It forms part of the toolkit of potential remedies which individual businesses can deploy themselves to restrain others from inappropriate market behaviour, without recourse to regulatory intervention. Formal intellectual property rights are effective, within their statutory definitions; but since trading models are infinitely various, there is still a need for the flexibility offered by purely common law remedies.

Why do we need a tort of passing off?

In a competitive, crowded marketplace, the temptation for a trader to get an advantage by suggesting to consumers that its goods or services are the same as, or related to, those of a successful competitor, is substantial. Once one trader's goods are recognised as good, or good value, then naturally consumers can be expected to seek those in preference to an unknown supplier's goods. This is true even if the unknown supplier's goods are as good as or even better than, its better known competitor's goods. Of course, many traders deal with this by spending large sums on advertising and other marketing activities. But some will succumb to the temptation to piggy-back on the success of an existing market leader.

Accordingly, all traders need to:

- identify their goods or services in such a way that consumers can easily differentiate them from competing offerings and
- police their market for any challenge to that differentiation.

One of the simplest and most effective ways to do so is branding: adopting a consistent sign which is used to promote the goods or services, which is unique to one trader. The sign may be a word, a logo, a colour scheme or distinctive packaging; in theory it may even be a sound (think of the Direct Line advertising jingle, or the once-ubiquitous Nokia phone ringtone) or a morphing image online. What matters is that it is distinctive and recognised by customers as indicating that the goods or services come from a particular trade source.

Registered trade marks: potential and limitations

The primary legal mechanism for protecting brands against imitation is to register them as trade marks. Registration, if available, puts the world on notice as to who has the legal right to use a particular sign on a particular category (or class) of goods or services, and entitles the trade mark owner to use the ® symbol on their goods to demonstrate that the sign is protected. It is relatively cheap, rapid and can be transferred to overseas markets thanks to a web of international laws and conventions: the European Union's Trade Marks Regulation and Directive (Regulation (EU) 2017/1001 and Directive (EU) 2015/2436), and the Madrid Agreement Concerning the International Registration of Marks. A registered trade mark is a form of property and so can be sold or used as security for debt; whereas there are no property rights in an unregistered brand in itself (although there may be property in the goodwill of the underlying business, and an unregistered brand can be assigned as part of that good will (Trade Marks Act s24(6))).

In short, if registration is available, it is an excellent mechanism and should be used. The first question to ask when a business complains about another's market behaviour is, what trade marks do you have registered? If a suitable registration exists, taking action for trade mark infringement is almost always going to be the cheapest and quickest way to stop the objectionable conduct. In extreme cases, the criminal law can also be invoked to stop registered trade mark infringement; and merely raising the possibility of criminal proceedings will bring most traders to reconsider their strategy.

What can be registered?

Most words or logos can be registered as trade marks, unless already registered for the same goods by someone else. But not all signs used in trade are capable of being registered at all. Many shapes, for instance, are liable to be refused registration on the grounds that consumers do not perceive them as brands – identifying the commercial source of the goods – but merely as the shape of the goods, or their container. Other signs, such as particular colours, may only be registered once they have been in use long enough for it to be demonstrable that they have achieved a high level of consumer recognition. But even then, defining the way in which the colour is to be used as a trade mark can be difficult to do sufficiently accurately, as Cadbury's recent loss of their registration of the purple shade long used on their Dairy Milk® range shows (*Cadbury UK Ltd v The Comptroller General of Patents, Designs and Trade Marks* [2018] EWCA Civ 2715).

How do marks come not to be registered?

Small businesses often do not anticipate the need to register their brands until they have become successful enough to be copied, or consider it but choose to spend the money on developing other aspects of their business. Equally, businesses which are expanding into the United Kingdom from overseas sometimes assume that the protection they have in their home market will extend to the UK without any further action on their own part, and are taken aback when it turns out that another business either is already using the same sign, or begins to do so once the launch publicity highlights it as a desirable brand. Alternatively, a trade mark may be registered for certain goods or services but a rival trader may start to use it for products for which is it not registered.

Consequently, the law needs to offer protection for brands which have not been registered.

Unfair competition

All signatories to the Paris Convention for the Protection of Industrial Property (which includes all members of the World Trade Organisation) are required to protect traders against such unfair competition. The Convention defines unfair competition as "any act of competition contrary to honest practices in industrial or commercial matters". The UK was instrumental in the drafting of this provision and is a signatory. But by unfortunate historical accident the principal action which is available in the UK goes by the confusing name of the tort of passing off, rather than the term unfair competition which is better recognised internationally and better conveys the plain English meaning.

The scope of the tort

Passing off is not limited only to the case where a trader uses another's brand on the packaging of goods, or in advertising services. Any form of deception of consumers as to an association between one trader's goods or services and another trader's business may fall within it. Over the years it has extended as the ways in which trade is carried on have evolved, and so can now be used to deal with situations such as untruthful suggestions of celebrity endorsement of goods, agency, authorised dealership or genuine merchandising, selling genuine but second-hand, reconditioned or low cost goods as first hand or premium quality, and so on. The common element is that some form of deception, whether deliberate or accidental, is taking place.

Generally it is the ultimate consumer being deceived, but deception of an intermediary in the chain can also constitute passing off. Reference to another trader's products is not, in itself, unlawful, and neither is successful honest competition no matter how strongly a first mover may feel that it has created a particular market and so has some kind of exclusive claim to it. The law of passing off comes into play only when the conduct of the newcomer is such as to mislead; but as soon as there is a realistic potential that someone is being or will be misled, then that conduct becomes actionable. This applies whether or not there is any intention to mislead.

The action exists to protect current business goodwill, and so is open only to those who can demonstrate that they are in business and have such goodwill. As well as traditional trading companies or sole traders, individuals with a commercial presence such as entertainers, artists and Instagram influencers can use passing off to prevent businesses from seeking to rise on their coattails. Unincorporated associations have the same rights in principle, although being unincorporated the action will need to be brought by one or more individual members on its behalf since an unincorporated association has no legal existence as a legal person.

If a misrepresentation is made which does not affect trading goodwill – for instance, a false statement that a rival successful trader learned the ropes from another now less successful enterprise, without suggesting any ongoing connection – then it is unlikely to be actionable. Similarly, a misrepresentation not made by a trader in the course of trade will not found a claim in passing off, although it could (depending on the facts) be an injurious falsehood, unlawful interference with business or even defamation. These causes of action are beyond the scope of this book.

Other possible remedies

Branding of a product may include a number of different components: a name is often the simplest and most prominent element, but there can be logos, a style of packaging, straplines and other advertising materials. These may be protected by rights including copyright and design right, depending upon what they are and how, where, when and by whom they were created. Accordingly, it is important to ascertain the full extent of the marketing which has been carried out for the product in question, and the full extent of similarities used by the imitator. Although a claim founded on these peripheral aspects may not achieve the objective of getting the product itself changed, it is likely to add pressure in any negotiations, and having to change all such aspects will add cost for the imitator which may assist in persuading them to change or at least modify the its branding.

CHAPTER TWO
ELEMENTS OF CLASSIC PASSING OFF

There is no statutory basis for the law of passing off. It has developed entirely through the common law over the last several centuries. As such, passing off suffers from the inevitable ambiguities resulting from different judges attempting to explain the analysis they have undertaken in their own words. The earlier cases are often reported very briefly, leaving multiple opportunities to infer differences in meaning where none may have been intended. But fortunately the senior courts have reviewed the issues thoroughly in relatively recent decisions, and earlier cases can now be treated as more or less authoritative according to how compatible they are with this recent analysis.

Goodwill, misrepresentation and damage

The current law derives from two House of Lords decisions: the *Advocaat* decision (*Erwin Warnink v Townend* [1979] All ER 927), and the *Jif Lemon* decision (*Reckitt & Colman v Borden* [1990] 1 All ER 873). Lord Diplock in *Advocaat* set out five characteristics which constitute the cause of action in passing off, which were subsequently condensed into three by Lord Oliver in *Jif Lemon*. These are:

- a ***misrepresentation*** which
- causes or is likely to cause ***damage*** to
- ***goodwill***.

Lord Diplock's characterisation emphasised in addition that the misrepresentation must be

- *made in the course of trade*, and
- *made to prospective or ultimate customers of the relevant goods or services.*

These additional factors are indeed still required, but in the majority of cases have not caused any difficulty and so need little discussion – although in the emerging commercial world of social media, questions around the addressee of material may in due course need to be asked. Instead, the courts' attention to date has been on issues raised in establishing the 'classical trinity' of misrepresentation, damage and goodwill. Each of these is the subject of a separate chapter, below.

Intention is irrelevant

It is important to stress that the misrepresentation need not have been made maliciously or fraudulently. One of the problems of dealing in intellectual property generally is that whereas the public at large well understands the principles of ownership when it comes to physical goods or land, relatively few people have the same sense of trespass when it comes to making use of someone else's idea, image or design. As a result, businesses frequently copy from each other with no sense of wrongdoing, and may respond with genuine disbelief when told that they have infringed any rights. At the other end of the scale, in particular in the case of supermarket lookalike products, a trader does know perfectly well that it is hoping to profit from sowing confusion among consumers, but has selected which design elements to copy with extreme care hoping to stay just the right side of the line. In neither case does this affect the application of the law, which requires only that a misrepresentation has been made and that damage has been suffered or is likely to be.

It follows that sincere good faith on the part of the party making the misrepresentation, including an honest belief in the truth of the statement, are no defence to a claim in passing off if in fact the statement does mislead customers.

Who can bring a claim

Passing off protects interests in trade, and so the status of both parties as traders is relevant to the analysis. It is not, however, necessary that the parties be direct competitors nor that the brand being imitated be particularly distinctive or even generally known. Passing off can be brought on the basis of a purely local reputation and goodwill – a well-established corner shop catering to a small town is entitled to protect its investment in building a business, just as much as a national chain with a vast advertising budget. The principle that "what is worth copying is worth protecting", though coined in relation to copyright, is just as applicable to passing off, with the caveat that unlike a claim for copyright infringement a claim in passing off may not protect a good brand on launch day: it has to have already attracted some goodwill.

These questions will also be reviewed in more detail in subsequent chapters.

CHAPTER THREE
THE CLAIMANT: GOODWILL

The heart of the tort of passing off is the need to protect the goodwill developed by a business among its customers over time.

What is goodwill?

Goodwill is "the benefit and advantage of the good name, reputation and connection of a business ... the attractive force which brings in custom" (*Inland Revenue Commissioners v Muller & Co's Margarine Ltd* [1901] AC 217). It is therefore inseparable from the business to which it adds value, which is why rights in an unregistered brand cannot be sold off separately from the underlying business, as a registered trade mark can be. It is therefore inaccurate to speak of a 'brand owner' in respect of unregistered brands; there is no property right in the brand as such, only in the goodwill of the business in which it is used. In this book the term 'branded business' is used to indicate the business using the brand and owning the associated goodwill.

Any functioning business, however small, which has customers is likely to possess at least some local goodwill, and therefore be able to bring an action to protect it. A tree surgery business operating locally within Surrey was able to obtain an injunction to stop a rival using a very similar name, although the injunction was stipulated to include only the GU,SL and KT postcodes but not the RG (Reading, Berkshire) area (*Redwood Tree Services Ltd v Warren Apsey t/a Redwood Tree Surgeons* [2011] EWPCC 14) .

The components making up goodwill can include the site of a particular shop, and the benefit of existing contracts with customers, but these cannot be damaged by a misrepresentation and so are not relevant for the purpose of a passing off claim. Any aspect which is capable of damage by misrepresentation can be relied upon. It is not necessary to break the business' goodwill into parts, such as a degree of recognition of the business name or product brand, and ascribe particular values to them, in order to demonstrate there has been damage to the goodwill as a whole. Conversely, a highly recognisable brand which is used by another trader in a commercial sector in which, for whatever reason, the brand originator has no current goodwill, cannot be protected by a claim in passing off. For instance, in *Harrods Ltd v Harrodian School Ltd* ([1996] RPC 697, CA) the famous department store was unable to prevent the launch of a new school under the name Harrodian because the store had no goodwill in any form of education, and so would not suffer any damage to its goodwill as a retailer from the alleged misrepresentation of a connection with the new enterprise.

Reputation is not necessarily goodwill

Although reputation is frequently a core element in proving the existence of goodwill, goodwill is legally a separate matter from reputation, which is a question of fact rather than a legal property right. This was the issue in the most recent case in passing off to have been decided by the UK Supreme Court, *Starbucks (HK) Ltd v BSkyB Group* ([2015] UKSC 31). The case concerned the trade mark NOW TV. The claimants, Starbucks (HK) Limited, are not the well-known coffee brand but the largest pay TV operator in Hong Kong under the brand NOW TV. When Sky announced that it was going to launch its own UK internet TV service, to be called NOW TV, Starbucks (HK) Ltd sued on the grounds that it had a sufficient reputation in the UK, gained via advertising and the internet even though no-one in the UK could receive Starbucks' NOW TV service. At the time, there were no UK-based subscribers and no equipment (i.e. set-top boxes) installed in the UK that could receive the service. The Supreme Court ruled that for there to be goodwill there must be active customers making a purchase of goods or services offered under the trade mark in the jurisdiction where passing off is alleged to have taken place. As there were no active customers in the UK and never had been, Starbuck (HK) Ltd's trade mark can have gained no goodwill in the UK despite some recognition by consumers.

This case appears to rule out as well the possibility of bringing a claim in passing off where a business is preparing to launch in the UK and so has some recognition here through advertising, directed at UK consumers, but has not yet begun to trade. Such pre-launch advertising may however enable a business to demonstrate the necessary goodwill within a very short time after actual trading begins (*MINERVA TM Reed Consumer Books Ltd v Pomaco Ltd* [2000] FSR 734), when simple preparation to trade (but without significant advertising) would not (*Hart v Relentless Records* [2002] FSR 35). Accordingly, an enterprise which finds its proposed brand being hijacked by another before launch should if possible both advertise and launch as quickly as possible in order to establish the necessary goodwill – although even this will not avoid a challenge if the rival enterprise is in good faith in using the same brand, perhaps in ignorance of the preparations which were being made.

It is possible for a business' goodwill to persist beyond the actual trading life of the enterprise, provided that the business has not been deliberately abandoned and there is some intention to recommence trading in the future. Such persistent goodwill may still have value and still found a claim in passing off – as for instance when a couturier who had been called up to serve in the army returned to business at the end of the First World War and successfully sued a business which had adopted his name (*Poiret v Jules Poiret* (1920) 37 RPC 177). In the long run, however, an intention to recommence will no longer sustain an action if the brand is no longer recognised by the target public.

Conversely, continued recognition of the brand by the public is not sufficient to maintain goodwill to found an action in passing off, if the business which originally developed the brand has conclusively ceased trading meanwhile. This was the case in *Barnsley Brewery Co Ltd v*

RBNB ([1997] FSR 462), where a beer known as Barnsley Bitter was fondly remembered by local consumers even 15 years after the brewery closed down – the point at which two rival businesses sought to revive the brand. What survived was only reputation, and even had the former brewery owner attempted to begin brewing and trading again, it would have to develop new goodwill on the back of its new endeavours.

It is also possible for a business with goodwill in the UK to be damaged by another passing off its goods in foreign markets, although the action is only likely to be effective if the business making the misrepresentations abroad has some form of presence in the UK in order for the court to seize jurisdiction.

Who can claim goodwill

Any party engaged in trade, whether as an individual or a corporate entity, is likely to be able to establish ownership of some form of goodwill. It is also possible for various kinds of clubs, associations, charities, public bodies, churches and so forth to enjoy goodwill, although it may be less self-evident whether any damage that such organisations suffer is to their trading goodwill. In such a case, a passing off action will fail. By way of example, the Law Society of England and Wales (a statutory body) has brought several successful passing off actions, as has the BBC; social clubs such as the British Legion, or sporting clubs such as Arsenal Football Club have also brought successful claims.

Individuals can bring a claim in passing off if they can demonstrate their professional or commercial status entitles them to the appropriate goodwill. For instance, in *Irvine v Talksport Ltd* ([2003] All ER 881) the racing driver Eddie Irvine successfully claimed damages against the newly launched Talksport Radio for sending out promotional flyers using his image, on the grounds that recipients were likely to assume that he was being paid to endorse the new service. However, adoption of another person's family name, or the name of their house, are not actionable since the use of such identifiers has no direct impact on the original bearer's ability to continue their professional or commercial activities under that name.

Trade and professional associations

Trade and professional associations have long been accepted to have standing to bring claims in passing off even without carrying on any trade in their own right. The types of claim which they can bring would include action against a person misrepresenting themselves as a member, or against a rival association misrepresenting itself as the claimant or asserting that its members can use the claimant's membership insignia. The basis for the claim is that the association has goodwill in the activity of conferring or withholding an endorsement, of qualification or membership, which could be damaged if another person or organisation appropriated the right to do so as well. However, a trade association representing the producers of a particular category of product – Scotch whisky, Parma ham or Swiss chocolate for instance – does not have standing to bring a passing off action on behalf of its members against a trader selling another product under a name or get up which suggests that it is the same category as its members' (e.g. selling chocolate, but not a form that meets the criteria necessary for being categorised as Swiss) (*Chocosuisse Union des Fabricants Suisse de Chocolat v Cadbury Ltd* 1999] RPC 826). This is because the trade association's interest in the matter – maintaining its own goodwill in the status of membership – is of an entirely different nature from its members' individual interest – in preventing sales of a product which unfairly trades on their goodwill in the high standard of their own product. Of course, if the association does actually sell products or services to the public in addition to maintaining the standard, along the lines of a producers' co-operative for example, then it has trading goodwill of the same kind as its members, and can bring the action.

Charities and other non-trading organisations

A charity which conducts any form of trade to raise funds, whether as a quasi-commercial operation such as the Oxfam shops or through occasional cake or jumble sales, will have trading goodwill and so be able to sustain an action in passing off to protect that goodwill. But not all charities trade in any sense whatsoever. A non-trading charity may nevertheless have sufficient goodwill in its fundraising activities to be able to bring a passing off action, whether against another charity using a confusingly similar name (*British Diabetic Association v The Diabetic Society* [1996] FSR 1), a sham charity or a commercial organisation holding itself out to be connected to the charity (*British Legion v British Legion Club (Street) Ltd* (1931) 48 RPC).

The Countryside Alliance, a non-political but non-charitable organisation, succeeded in an action to prevent a non-member standing for election to a local council and purporting to be their candidate (*Burge v Haycock* ([2001] EWCA Civ 900). However, this case is very much a borderline one since the action of the bogus candidate did not directly threaten the Alliance's fundraising interest. In other interest group cases, actions in defamation (*Pryce v Pioneer Press* (1925) 42 TLR 29) or copyright infringement (*Kennard v Lewis* [1983] FSR 346) have been brought; and a claim based on a combination of causes of action may be the best approach.

Ownership of goodwill

Since trading has moved beyond the model under which a craftsman made and then sold individual items direct to consumers, the issue of goodwill has to take into account the multiple stages through which a modern product comes to be produced and marketed. Several businesses may be involved, and consequently disagree as to ownership of the whole or a share of the goodwill that consumers bear towards the product. Where the goods are marketed as those of a particular supplier, then the issue is straightforward: the business with which consumers associate the product owns the goodwill. This applies equally to businesses operating on a franchised basis: the public may realise that different outlets are run by different businesses, but they will expect that standards are determined by the entity which licenses the use of the brand.

But there are many categories of product, such as cards or posters, for which consumers have no particular interest in identifying the supplier since they select a product entirely on aesthetic grounds. In other categories, functionality or even price may be the consumers' focus. In such cases it is necessary to establish which party is most responsible for the character or quality of the goods at the point of sale, as a matter of fact. A manufacturer which sells a non-standard product through multiple dealers is more likely to be recognised as the owner of goodwill than one selling a product where the dealer also stocks substitutable alternatives. The outcome will be a question of fact in each case, and the conclusion not necessarily easy to foresee. For this reason, in a supply chain agreements dealing with the ownership of prospective goodwill between traders are advisable and commonplace. Any brand licensing arrangement should include such a provision, since it will not only formalise the legal position but also ensure that the licensee undertakes its obligations in the knowledge that goodwill arising from its marketing efforts will accrue to the licensor – a situation which licensees commonly fail to appreciate, if it is not spelled out.

A foreign manufacturer which does not sell on its own account in the UK can still acquire UK goodwill through a licensee's efforts provided the foreign company is recognised as the ultimate source of the goods (*MedGen Inc v Passion for Life Products Ltd* [2001] FSR 30). If the foreign origin of the goods is concealed, or simply not made known, then absent any contractual provision to the contrary, the UK licensee will own the resulting goodwill (*Scandecor Development AB v Scandecor Marketing AB* [1999] 26 CA). Even if the goods are known to be imported, the public trust in the importer's ability to select and handle goods to a particular standard may lead to this outcome.

It is not necessary for customers to know the actual identity of the business, or they may know it only by a trading name rather than a legal identity, provided that they recognise the products or services as having a single trade origin and are concerned to buy from that source (*United Biscuits (UK) Ltd v Asda Stores Ltd* [1997] RPC 513).

An employee will not generally own any goodwill in the business which employs them, even if the business bears their family name (*Asprey & Garrard Ltd v WRA (Guns) Ltd and Asprey* (2001] EWCZ Civ 1499].

A partnership, unlike an unincorporated association, can own goodwill and accordingly the changes of partners do not affect the ownership, nor do individual partners normally acquire any personal interest in it (*Byford v Oliver* [2003] EWHC 295). Expiry of a partnership agreement without provision for sale of the business can, nevertheless, lead to the former partners being entitled to continue to trade, separately, under the brand of the former partnership (*Burchell v Wilde* [1900] 1 Ch 551 CA) – although clearly this is not a good idea.

Dealings in goodwill

As personal property, goodwill can be assigned or pass through inheritance either under a will or on intestacy, or by operation of law on insolvency. But it is not capable of being dealt with separately from the business in which it arises. Provided that this restriction is observed, goodwill can be assigned by contract in any form recognised by law; it need not be in writing, signed or specifically state that the goodwill element of the business is included. A sale of a business as a whole will necessarily include the goodwill pertaining to it, and a transaction in the brands used with particular goods or services will include the goodwill associated with their use. Agreements which attempt the converse – a sale of goodwill without a business, or a licence of marks without any business association – are unlikely to be legally effective (*Pinto v Badman* (1981) 8 RPC 181, CA). A transaction which splits an existing business between separate owners can effectively split the goodwill formerly associated with the business as a whole, provided that to do so would not result in any deception of the public (*Star Industrial Co Ltd v Yap Kwee Kor* [1976] FSR 256, PC).

Once goodwill has been assigned, the seller may set up in direct competition but by implied agreement may not solicit customers of the previous business, unless the contrary is agreed (*Trego v Hunt* [1896] AC 7). The non-solicitation obligation does not preclude advertising to the public at large, which may of course lead to former customers being attracted to the new business; the seller may, if so, continue to deal with them. If the buyer wishes to avoid such competition, it must include an express non-compete provision (although this will need careful drafting if not to fall foul of the normal prohibition on restraint of trade).

Goodwill may in some circumstances inure to particular business premises, such as a pub. If so, then an assignment of the lease or freehold may be effective to transfer the goodwill of a business formerly trading from that address; the purchaser is under no obligation to change the property name, or to use an assumed name rather than the physical address, merely because a former occupant has developed goodwill and continues to trade elsewhere. This will not necessarily extend to using the name as a brand on goods, however (*Rickerby v Reay* (1903) 20 RPC 380).

A transaction under which a personal name, the same as a known brand, is licensed by someone whose own name it is to a business for that business to use in competition with the known brand, will be ineffective as a defence against a claim for passing off brought by the owner of the established brand business (*Dunhill v Sunoptic* [1979] FSR 337). The transaction is in reality a form of attempted fraud.

Goodwill as security for debt

As property, goodwill can be and frequently is mortgaged or charged as part of a company debenture, although its value in this context is limited since the mortgagee, which is not trading the business itself, acquires no right to enforce any unregistered brands through a passing off action. The mortgage documents should therefore include the obligation on the mortgagor to take such an action should the mortgagee require it. Suitable safeguards such as a requirement to take an opinion from suitable counsel before invoking such a clause should also be included, since the bank or other lender is unlikely to have the expertise to assess when such a claim can succeed, in an unfamiliar field of commerce or industry.

Remedies for non-traders

The absence of goodwill of the appropriate (commercial) kind is not an absolute bar to bringing a claim, merely to a claim in passing off.

If a misrepresentation is made which directly and naturally harms a person's economic interests, such as their employment prospects, an action in injurious falsehood may be possible provided that the false statement has been made "maliciously", in the sense that "the words were calculated to produce damage and that the defendant knew when he published the words that they were false or was reckless as to whether they were false or not" (*Kaye v Robertson* [1991] FSR 62).

A person whose name is used by another in connection with a business, thereby exposing them to potential liability, is entitled to restrain that use. This arises for instance in connection with partners retiring from a partnership, and could be invoked where a person who (unlike Eddie Irvine) is not engaged in commerce is cited as endorsing a product or business.

Depending upon the form of the misrepresentation, claims in defamation, copyright infringement or breach of confidence could also be brought to bear.

CHAPTER FOUR THE CLAIMANT: DAMAGE

In any potential dispute, it makes sense to assess at the outset whether the party feeling aggrieved has suffered any damage. If there is nothing to recover, then bringing a claim is a costly way of salving a bruised ego. But in passing off, notwithstanding a well-established business, and an outrageous misrepresentation, the cause of action cannot be made out unless it can be shown that there is a genuine likelihood of damage to the business. "Mere confusion which does not lead to a sale is not sufficient" (*Reckitt & Colman Products Ltd v Borden Inc* [1990] 1 All ER 873).

Types of damage

There are two possible forms of damage to the goodwill of a business. The first is a diminution in value due to reduction in the goodwill itself – for example, because the rival business sells poorer quality goods leading customers to lower their opinion of the brand owner (that is to say, the owner of the established business using the brand). Less critically, but economically just as undesirable and more common in practice, is simple loss of business due to sales being made by the rival business which would otherwise have been made by the branded business. This diversion of business will reduce sales, and therefore damage the profitability of the business, and is thus actionable even if the rival business is selling superior goods which might, left unchallenged, ultimately lead to an improvement in the reputation of the brand.

Indeed, the need for damage is also helpful in discriminating between misrepresentations which are actionable and those that are not: a misrepresentation of a kind which does not foreseeably cause damage will not be actionable, however annoying it may be. A good example is the long-running dispute over the beer brand Budweiser. As a result of events in the Second World War two separate businesses had equally good faith claims to the brand. The Court of Appeal held that the American brewer Anheuser-Busch (whose sales in the UK were purely to American servicemen at US bases) faced no risk of damage to its goodwill as a result of sales of the identically branded beer to the rest of the UK market by the original Czech brewer, Budejovicky Budvar (*Anheuser-Busch Inc v Budejovicky Budvar NP* [1984] FSR 413).

There is no need for actual damage to be proved so long as it can be shown to be realistically likely. To hold otherwise would prevent claimants from bringing action promptly as soon as the misrepresentation is made. But in such circumstances, the branded business' owner will not recover more than nominal damages; the real prize is an injunction to prevent the misrepresentation from being repeated or continued.

Can damage be assumed?

Damage may be effectively assumed where the passing off taking place is the classic form of a misrepresentation that the goods or services sold by the defendant are those of the branded business' owner. Unless such a misrepresentation is totally incredible on its face for some reason, it is obvious that some consumers will buy from the defendant *because* they would otherwise have bought from the branded business. But mere evidence of consumer confusion is not sufficient to prove damage. Consumers are often and easily confused, particularly where low value goods are concerned since most people do not pay close attention when buying household staples, for example. Consumers must, instead, be deceived as to the goods' nature or origin, and this must result from the defendant's use of a brand being taken by consumers as a representation of connection with the branded business owner (*Premier Luggage and Bags v Premier Co* [2002] EWCA Civ 387). Indeed, even if a consumer can be shown to have bought the defendant's goods believing them to be the branded business owner's, this does not show that the consumer bought them *because* they believed them to be the branded business owner's. They may have been entirely indifferent as to whose goods they bought, taking the view that most of the alternatives on offer were equivalent, and simply happened to have believed them to originate from the brand. The goodwill of the brand must have been effective in bringing about the sale; only in those circumstances does such a sale constitute damage to the branded business.

Where a sale is made business to business, for instance from a supplier to a retailer, the retailer is likely to be more expert at discriminating between brands and copies than a consumer would normally be. It can therefore be that the retailer is not deceived by the product's name and appearance into thinking that it is the branded original. Nonetheless, if the get-up is such that consumers are likely to be deceived when the retailer puts them on sale, a claim for passing off can be brought even at this early stage, the products themselves being "instruments of deception" (discussed further in Chapter 6 below). This applies whether the products are to be put on the market in the UK or exported abroad.

Unimportance of fraud in a claim for passing off

If the seller can be shown to have acted fraudulently, it is not necessary to show actual diversion of sales or damage to goodwill: the seller's intent to profit by deception effectively bars it from claiming to have failed to do so (*Lever v Goodwin* [1887] 36 ChD 1). But even if it is apparent that the seller really did fail to deceive anyone, it is still arguable that damage can be inferred from the effort to deceive. First, an honest person would have been prepared to pay for a licence, and secondly the defendant's dishonest practices may in one way or another damage the branded business owner's good reputation. However, given that fraud is not a necessary component for a claim to succeed, and that it can be an expensive and time-consuming issue to prove, as a matter of practicality it may not be worth invoking unless ample and convincing (rather than circumstantial) evidence is available at the outset. This is rarely the case. Frequently a trader, faced with what it considers an unconscionable attempt to copy its brand and profit from its goodwill, leaps to a conclusion that deliberate and fraudulent intent is to blame, and thereafter sees evidence for that intent in every piece of information obtained. But on an objective view, proof of fraud requires more than mere copying (which the defendant may not have considered improper) and competition. It may require correspondence or internal documents stating in terms that the object of creating a similar-looking product is not merely to *attract* customers but to *deceive* them. Such documents are not often forthcoming.

Heads of damage

The simplest form of damage is direct loss of sales. Once a rival seller has launched and can be shown to be diverting sales which the branded business would otherwise have made, then the accompanying loss of profits from those sales is sufficient damage to sustain an action. This is true even if the parties are targeting separate markets (expensive versus low cost goods, for instance).

Where the rival seller is targeting a lower cost market, and selling inferior goods, even if no actual loss of sales is likely the loss of reputation (actual or feared) is damage to goodwill, and will found a claim in passing off. If the defendant is selling an inferior category of the branded business' goods as a superior category, the same applies despite the fact both are the branded business' own goods: the loss of control of the marketing to maintain the separate markets makes it foreseeable that the goodwill in the business of the superior goods will be damaged in time.

A defendant which is not in direct competition with the branded business may still cause damage, if the business it is carrying on is intrinsically disreputable (as when the Mayfair night club Annabel's sued to prevent an escort agency from using the name (*Annabel's v Schock* [1972] RPC 838) or if the defendant itself has a poor reputation or a history of repeated breaches of the law or insolvencies. A claim based on this kind of damage will need to establish good grounds for the allegations, and for asserting that a significant fraction of the public will in some way hold the branded business responsible. Even if the defendant has no such negative connotations for the brand at present, the fact that the branded business has no control over its use of the brand, and is therefore being forced to trust its reputation to an unknown third party, could be said to constitute a future risk of damage. But this argument is very weak unless some grounds exist to show that the risk is more than speculative, and should perhaps be invoked only as a second string to more robust heads of damage.

A claim to be an authorised dealer of the branded business is objectionable not only because of the deception involved, but also because consumers may seek compensation for faulty goods from the branded business. While such claims are unlikely to succeed, the cost and time of dealing with them, and the loss of goodwill among the public at large from appearing to repudiate one's own products, constitute an additional head of damage.

Damage suffered to the branded business' trade relationships can also be claimed. This arises where, for instance, the defendant is late paying debts or fails to respond to correspondence, leading to retailers or suppliers blaming the branded business for the defendant's poor conduct (*Chelsea Man Menswear v Chelsea Girl* [1987] RPC 187). Passing off seconds or discontinued products as the current range can also cause the branded business' suppliers to believe they are being treated unfairly on terms. Similarly, damage may be caused by a claim to be licensed by the branded business since it may lose the branded business an opportunity to grant a genuine licence, or cause existing licensees to reconsider their association with the brand, if the defendant is disreputable. If the branded business does grant licences, then it may be possible to claim damages on the basis of the royalties that the defendant ought to have agreed to pay.

Use of a known brand in a field closely related to that in which the brand is established may foreclose a future opportunity for the branded business to expand into that field. An example might be a leisure clothing brand being adopted by another trader to use in specialist outdoor gear. Clearly, this will cause concern, but unless the two fields are very closely connected it will not always cause damage if the branded business had no credible intention of launching in the ancillary field. Any other principle would give brands too wide a monopoly to prevent use of a brand indefinitely, without any need to trade in related fields themselves.

Loss of exclusivity in relation to a brand does not normally constitute a separate head of damage, but could do under some rare circumstances such as where a large and well-known enterprise adopts a brand already in use by a smaller concern. The new entrant is unlikely to damage the reputation of the brand as such, but it may in time lead to the smaller enterprise being seen as the usurper and so losing its own good reputation (*Provident Financial v Halifax Building Society* [1994] FSR 81).

There are no such rare circumstances, however, under which mere dilution of the exclusivity of a brand will amount to sufficient damage to bring an action. Dilution refers to the position where a brand is not only exclusive within a particular market, but across a wide range of markets. For such a brand, its sheer uniqueness adds to its value since consumers will be likely always to associate it with only the owner's products and services. But if a new trader adopts the brand for use in a market for totally unrelated goods and services, and without in any way suggesting that there is an association with the original brand, it is highly unlikely that any misrepresentation is being made nor that any tangible damage will be suffered. Consumers are sophisticated enough to understand that different enterprises use the same or similar brands, and will not attribute the products or conduct of one enterprise to the other. The term dilution is frequently heard in discussions of branding, but this is because it is a statutory head of loss under the US law of trademarks. The English courts have repeatedly refused to recognise it as a head of damage in passing off.

CHAPTER FIVE
THE CUSTOMERS' PERCEPTIONS: WHAT CONSTITUTES A MISREPRESENTATION

No action in passing off will succeed unless there can be shown to have been a misrepresentation. The misrepresentation could be made in words, but rarely is; most frequently, a mark or get-up of a product is copied or imitated, and the implication that the goods or services to which these are applied are those of the brand owner (the owner of the established business using the brand) is left to be taken by consumers. But the use must be such as is likely to mislead, in all the circumstances. An unregistered mark or brand is not a monopoly; other traders are free to use the same or very similar brands, provided that in the marketplace concerned customers are not going to be misled. This is an important difference from the rights conferred by a registered trade mark. The branded business' rights are not property rights in the mark itself, but in the goodwill of the underlying business.

Accordingly, another trader using the same mark, but in such a way that there is no damage to the original's business is unlikely to appropriate any goodwill from the branded business, and cannot be said to be passing off its goods as those of the brand. For instance, a bicycle repair shop in Lands End is unlikely to cause customers to leave the similarly named one in Berwick on Tweed; or use of the same sign as a brand for cosmetics is unlikely to affect the original brand as a purveyor of sporting equipment. Fair use of a rival's brand in a comparative advert, or to indicate that the two sets of goods are substitutable or capable of being used as spares are not liable to damage the brand's goodwill. Nor will purely satirical reference, or mere advertising puffery as to the superiority of the defendant's goods, be likely to meet the standard for an actionable misrepresentation.

Statements to indicate that a commercial relationship has existed in the past are not misrepresentations (if true) and so not actionable in passing off. The way to restrain such references after termination of the relationship is through contractual terms.

Still less do misrepresentations about the branded business as such, rather than any connection with the defendant's goods or business, constitute passing off. If anything, they may be actionable as injurious falsehood.

An omission can amount to misrepresentation, such as an offering of the defendant's own goods in response to a request for the branded product, without further explanation. However, traders do not have any responsibility for correcting mistakes made by consumers themselves. If a consumer is familiar with only one manufacturer for a particular category of goods, and so assumes that any goods in that category originate from that manufacturer, the trader is under no duty to point the misconception out.

A claim to a characteristic of the goods, such as an accreditation or regulatory approval, which the branded goods do possess but which the defendant's do not, can amount to a misrepresentation (*SDS Biotech UK Ltd v Power Agrichemicals Ltd* [1995] FSR 797). Similarly, a claim that a product, made from the branded parts but assembled by the rival business, is the branded product is actionable (*Richards v Williamson* (1874) 30 LT 746).

A thorough assessment of all the circumstances is therefore necessary, to determine whether the use is likely to mislead, or not. Of course, if the name, type of goods and get up are all copied exactly then it will be obvious. But few cases are quite so clear cut.

The relevance of truth

A statement can be a misrepresentation even though it is, on absolutely objective terms, true. This startling conclusion arises from a 19th century case concerning an industrial fabric known as camel hair belting but believed by all concerned not to be made from actual camel hair. By independent expert analysis it was found that it was, in fact, made of camel hair. The court nevertheless held that the defendant's use of the term camel hair belting was a misrepresentation, not as to the substance of the fabric but as to the commercial source (*Reddaway v Banham* [1896] AC 199).

The question is therefore not whether there is an objectively true interpretation which the statement can bear, and which the defendant perhaps intended it to bear, but what effect the statement will have on the minds of customers. If it will deceive a substantial proportion then even if the rest are not misled, it may be actionable. Once again, the question of the defendant's honesty is beside the point: the issue is whether the statement in fact misleads, not whether it was intended to do so. Consequently, a statement which is objectively false, and is even intended to mislead, will not constitute passing off if in all the circumstances it cannot deceive anyone. The *Parma Ham* case concerned pre-packaged sliced ham. This, simply by reason of being pre-packaged, could be seen not to be Parma ham in the sense (of being sliced from the whole ham, in front of the buyer at the time of purchase) relied upon by the Italian Parma Ham Consortium in their passing off claim (*Consorzio del Prosciutto di Parma v Marks & Spencer plc* [1991] RPC 351, CA). There was therefore no material misrepresentation in labelling it Parma ham, when in fact the packets contained ham made and sliced in Parma.

Cases such as this raise a question as to whether consumers actually know what the definition of a product such as Parma ham is, in order to be deceived or otherwise. Other cases have dealt with Swiss chocolate, or champagne – premium products which the public know and appreciate, but are unlikely to be able to define with any precision.

Nonetheless, the courts have been prepared to uphold passing off claims following evidence as to the nature of the product the public are familiar with regardless of the letter of any regulations determining how the product is legally required to be made (*Chocosuisse v Cadbury Ltd* [1999] RPC 826, CA; *J Bollinger SA v Costa Brava Wine Co Ltd* [1961] 3 All ER 561).

Materiality

If a misrepresentation is not such as to influence a consumer's decision, then even if the consumer is deceived the misrepresentation is not actionable. No damage has arisen from the error.

Time of making the statement

A specific question as to the materiality of the misrepresentation concerns statements which are made at some time other than the immediate point of sale. Clearly, a misrepresentation made after the transaction is complete cannot possibly have had any effect on the customer's choice. A false statement made well before the transaction may have been forgotten or corrected by the time the customer comes to buy, and if so does not harm the branded business' goodwill. But it will be difficult to establish what, if any effect, such a misrepresentation has, and the further before the purchase the statement is made, the less clear-cut its connection with the decision to buy will be.

'Free' goods

Even if the reader or other consumer does not hand over money, the costs of free newspapers and other such enterprises must be found from somewhere whether through advertisers or investors. Competition for such sources of funding is fierce. The fact that any misrepresentation is addressed to the readers rather than to the funders is immaterial: the misrepresentation is still made, and made in a trading context (*Tam-*

worth Herald v Thomson Free Newspapers [1991] FSR 337). Indeed, in the case of free newspapers the connection between readership and advertising revenue is close and so it scarcely matters whether the readers or the advertisers are considered to be the publisher's customers. Similarly, an online jobs site on which employment candidates could list without charge, but which was funded by the businesses which advertised their vacancies there, was successfully sued for passing off because it was demonstrated that the candidates were confused as to the identity of the business behind the website although the payers were not (*Reed Executive plc v Reed Business Information Ltd* [2002] EWHC 367).

Give-away software may likewise not be a direct source of revenue but is likely (if useful!) to be a source of goodwill (*Jian Tools for Sales Inc v Roderick Manhattan Group Ltd* [1995] FSR 924).

Disclaimers and co- or own-branding

A trader hoping to benefit from drawing customers' attention to an existing brand in connection with its own goods might consider that the danger of being sued for passing off could be negated by including a suitable disclaimer in its advertising, packaging or otherwise. However, the court's view is that such disclaimers hardly ever work: customers may not see or take note of them, and even those who do may conclude that the remaining use of the brand was authorised on condition of printing the disclaimer (*Associated Newspapers Group plc v Insert Media Ltd* [1990] 2 All ER 803). To overcome such reasoning the disclaimer would need to be clear, so prominent as to be unmissable and wholly unambiguous. The use of the name Andrex on promotional packs of the rival product Nouvelle was held to be passing off even though the form of use was as a legitimate comparator ("Softness guaranteed (or we'll exchange it for Andrex)"), because the prominence of the famous name Andrex was such that a substantial number of consumers would be deceived, taking no notice of the actual brand name or small disclaimer (*Kimberley-Clark Ltd v Fort Sterling Ltd* [1997] FSR 877).

Similarly, a trader which applies a name, logo or get-up to a product intending to reference an existing brand may also use its own name on the product and packaging, aiming to distinguish the goods from the branded product. But this is only likely to be effective if the similarity of the branding is not so close as to mislead consumers as to the source of the goods. Again, consumers buying low cost goods spare little attention to questions of origin and so need very clear explanation that what they are buying is different from the branded original. Although 'own brands' are now very common in supermarkets such that customers are familiar with the concept, they are also aware that originators do sometimes manufacture goods to be sold as own brands and may still draw an inference as to an association between the products of one kind or another.

Wording such as "similar to" the brand, or "[X] type" may be enough to clarify that the goods supplied will not be the branded ones themselves, but as with the Andrex case a rival trader needs to be very careful and clear in its usage to ensure that no unintended misrepresentation is made (*Broad & Co Ltd v Cast Iron Drainage Co Ltd* [1970] FSR 363).

CHAPTER SIX
THE DEFENDANT: TRADERS, OFFICERS, OTHERS

The *Jif Lemon* requirement that the misrepresentation causes damage to the trading goodwill of the owner of the established business using the brand implies, but does not strictly require, that the party making the misrepresentation must itself be in some way connected with trade. Lord Diplock in *Advocaat* made this requirement express, but there have nonetheless been cases where the trading status of the maker of the misrepresentation was borderline. The ordinary case does of course concern two businesses competing for the same customers; but this is by no means the limit.

Misrepresentation by non-competitors

Occasionally misrepresentations are made by enterprises which are not in fact trading in competition with the branded business. Some of these fall clearly into the category of frauds, as where a party claims payment for the branded goods or services without any intention or attempt to supply them. In other cases, the name of a shell company may be changed or a website set up in the name of a well-known brand, in the hope that the branded business will offer a sum of money for transfer of the company or site.

Cybersquatting

In the online form this is known as cybersquatting. The courts were originally sympathetic to applications for the change of the name or transfer to the branded business (*British Telecommunications plc v One in a Million Ltd* [1999] 1 WLR 903). Whether the cause of action in such a case is properly passing off or purely the tort of deceit is arguable. The courts have come close to concluding that the existence on the relevant register of a name to the use of which the defendant has no rights amounts, in itself, to a representation to the public which is calculated to damage the goodwill of the branded business. In reality, members of the public are unlikely to be aware of such registers let alone any entries on them, and the impact on the branded business' goodwill would be difficult if not impossible to establish unless and until the registrant performs some further act. At most, the holder of a misleadingly named domain which could be used as a channel for passing off goods and services, could be required to surrender it under the principle of equitable protection but it gives rise to no claim in damages. This more careful approach was confirmed by the Court of Appeal in *Media Agency Group Ltd v Space Media Agency Ltd* ([2019] EWCA Civ 712): both goodwill and a misrepresentation must be proved in order to succeed in a claim for passing off.

Non-trading entities

But beyond the category of defendants who are not trading in anything at all, there are entities such as community groups or charities which may not carry on a formal trade. The branded business will need to demonstrate that the misrepresentation complained of had some connection with trade rather than being merely a falsehood or disparagement more appropriately dealt with through another cause of action.

The distributor of free newspapers and other goods is nonetheless in the course of trade unless entirely funded from philanthropic sources.

Non-competing traders

Where the party making the misrepresentation is a trader, though one which operates in a different field, the lack of common activity is no bar to a claim in passing off. In *Harrods Ltd v Harrodian School Ltd* ([1886] RPC 697) the famous department store attempted to prevent the defendant school, which was being set up on a sports ground which the store had formerly owned and run for its staff, from using the name Harrodian. The claim failed, but only because the store failed to show any damage from the operation of a school under that name, not as a matter of law.

Of course, if the parties operate in totally separate spheres then the risk that any customers will be misled into thinking there is any connection must be lower, and the more so the further apart those fields of activity are. But the principle that a trader making a misrepresentation may be liable in passing off, if damage can be shown, remains. A really famous brand will naturally have more chance of demonstrating the risk exists even in a fairly distinct field than one known only to local customers or customers for a specialist kind of goods. Thus for instance the British Medical Association were able to prevent a retail chemist using the initials BMA (*British Medical Association v Marsh* (1931) 48 RPC 565) and the tobacco brand Alfred Dunhill prevented an unrelated company using the name Dunhills for sunglasses (*Alfred Dunhill Ltd v Sunoptic SA* [1979] FSR 337, CA).

Misrepresentations to suppliers

Since a business' goodwill may include goodwill with its suppliers, a misrepresentation made not to customers but to suppliers can also be passing off. The degree of deceptiveness may need to be higher, since in general terms businesses can be assumed to take greater care to ascertain who they are dealing with than consumers do. But the principle is identical.

Liable parties

The trader itself, shareholders and directors

In the majority of passing off cases, the party making a misrepresentation is a trader making it to the end user of the goods or services. If so, it is that trader which is liable for any damage resulting to the branded business.

Potentially, where a limited company is concerned which is in effect the *alter ego* of an individual shareholder and director, its sole director may also be liable under the normal rules of joint liability. This requires the director to be so closely identifiable with the acts of the company that they can be said to have procured or induced the acts which are found to have constituted passing off. A director, even the sole one of a corporate entity, will not normally be jointly liable for its actions if all they have done is carry out duties entrusted to them by the company through normal constitutional arrangements (*Sea Shepherd UK v Fish and Fish Ltd* [2015] UKSC 10). But in the case of a 'one man company' an evidential presumption may arise that such that a director who actively co-operates with a company to bring about the infringing activity and intended that their co-operation would help to bring the act about can be jointly personally liable with the company (*Grenade (UK) Ltd v Grenade Energy Ltd* [2016] EWHC 877 (IPEC)).

Manufacturers and supply chain: 'instruments of deception'

Other participants in the supply chain can also be liable, including manufacturer, importers and wholesalers. But these intermediaries are only likely to be liable in the special case where the products themselves are inherently likely to deceive ultimate purchasers, and so can be considered in themselves to be 'instruments of deception'. In such circumstances, even though none of the suppliers in the chain from manufacturer to retailer are themselves deceived as to the nature or source of the goods, any party selling the goods could be liable for passing off – even though the final end-user sale and actual deception do not take place until a later date.

This possibility can arise to a greater or lesser degree of likelihood in a number of different circumstances.

Where goods are made or packaged to be so similar to the branded product that it is inherently likely consumers will be deceived unless specific efforts are made to avoid this at the point of final sale, then each supplier in the chain will be jointly liable for passing off even if unaware that such a deception will take place. The act of putting such deceptive goods into circulation is sufficient to constitute passing off, and an injunction and nominal damages can be obtained to prevent further such sales.

Such blatantly infringing products are however not the norm. More usually, the goods are or are packaged to be similar to the branded product, but to the extent that a discerning buyer could find out that they are not. Others may be somewhat similar but unlikely to deceive unless the context or another circumstance assists in leading the buyer to the belief that they are associated with the brand. Sale of such potentially – but not necessarily – deceptive goods may not amount to passing off at the point of consumer sale unless the retailer makes some further effort to misrepresent them as the branded product. Sale of the goods by an intermediary in the supply chain will not in these circumstances be passing off as such, but the supplier could be a joint tortfeasor if it realises and intends or accepts that the ultimate retailer will use the goods to pass them off to the end buyer. Of course, there will be a range of deceptiveness in this category of goods: some may deceive all but the most careful of buyers, while others may bear only a passing similarity to the branded goods so that only the truly distracted are deceived.

For this category, a detailed consideration of both the degree of deceptiveness of the goods and what awareness the supplier had of the retailer's business activities will be needed in order to establish liability.

The branded business owner will need to demonstrate that the supplier knew the goods were going to be used dishonestly and was contributing to that. There will also need to be an assessment of the extent to which retailers are indeed using the goods to pass them off; if this is only an occasional and small scale occurrence, with most of the products being sold honestly, then it will be harder to argue that a dealer's co-operation in such limited activities is enough to demonstrate that the goods themselves are instruments of deception. In practice, it will always be prudent to allege that a supplier is liable in the alternative, both for passing off and as a joint tortfeasor in the passing off carried out by the retailer.

In the third category, a supplier may not handle the goods themselves but only contribute labels or packaging which are applied to the goods by another. Once again, liability will depend upon the degree of deceptiveness of these materials and the complicity or ignorance of the supplier, and joint tortfeasorship is likely to be the appropriate form of claim alongside the retailer with primary liability for passing off.

Conversely, a trader which supplies staple commercial products to another which then uses them for passing off will not be liable, even if it knows that they are to be used for that purposes, unless acting in a common design with the other party as a joint tortfeasor. Merely selling standard products can never amount to passing off since they are not instruments of deception themselves.

It is also worth noting that a supplier of means to potentially create deceptive goods will not be liable for passing off if their goods cannot come to the end consumer's attention. In *Apollinaris Co v Duckworth* ((1906) 23 RPC 540 CA) the complaint concerned Apollinaris Water, a naturally occurring German mineral water which in Edwardian times was the largest selling mineral water in the world (even having a walk-on part in James Joyce's *Dubliners*). The defendant sold packets of salts which were labelled to show they could be used, with water, to make up an imitation of the natural product. The English licensee of genuine Apollinaris Water sued to prevent their distribution. But any purchaser of these packets of salts would necessarily know they were not buying Apollinaris Water itself. Conversely, no customer who bought a drink stated to be Apollinaris Water but which was in fact the imitation version would ever have seen the label on the salts. As a result, the defendant was not passing off. The same conclusion applies if the dealer uses the brand in price lists circulated to the trade, but not on the products themselves, so that retailers must deliberately choose to label the products with the brand or otherwise promote them as such, in order for any customer to be deceived (*Star Cycles v Frankenbergs* (1907) RPC 405 CA).

Exporters

If goods which are inherently instruments of deception are exported from the UK, the exporter is liable for passing off provided it can be shown that buyers in the destination market will be deceived. Thus for instance, if the brand is unknown in the destination market, the export will not constitute passing off. Note that it is not necessary to show that the sales would infringe any rights as a matter of local law in the destination market. It may be that they do, which may give rise to a further cause of action, but this is not necessary to the analysis under passing off for the action in the UK.

A more complex issue arises where the UK exporter sells the means with which to commit deception in another market – as for instance, bulk Scotch whisky, bottles, stoppers and labels, knowing that the importer in the country of destination will mix the whisky with local spirits before filling the bottles and selling the result as Scotch. The case law here is consistent in finding that the exporter can be injuncted, but less consistent as to the legal basis for this. If the sales in the destination market breach any local law, the exporter is plainly liable as a joint tortfeasor with the importer at destination. But if the destination market does not, or is not proved to have, any law against such mixing, then the court appears to be holding that the whisky is itself an instrument of deception (*John Walker v Douglas McGibbon* [1975] RPC 506; *John Walker v Henry Ost* [1970] RPC 489) – which, in its pure, if bulk form, it cannot realistically be (*British Telecommunications plc v One in a Million* [1999] FSR 1, CA).

CHAPTER SEVEN THE PRODUCT AS A MISREPRESENTATION: DISTINCTIVENESS AND DECEPTION

The most common forms of misrepresentation replied upon in claims for passing off are signs: a name, logo, packaging get-up or other indication which is said to be deceptively similar to the branded product. But the claim depends on whether or not this branding is, in reality, distinctive of the brand owner (the owner of the established business in which the brand is used). If it is not distinctive, then another's use of it cannot be effective as a misrepresentation and so cannot harm the brand. This is one of the important ways in which a claim for passing off differs from one for trade mark infringement. If a mark is on the register, it can be infringed. But a product name, look and get-up which is in use but is not inherently distinctive and has not become so through sufficient use and advertising, cannot found a claim in passing off. It follows that disputes frequently centre on whether or not the claimant's brand was, in fact, distinctive.

Copying does not prove distinctiveness

The fact, if proven, that the rival trader has chosen to copy the branding does tend to support the argument that it was in some degree distinctive, and help to sway the court in a case where other factors are finely balanced. But it is important not to rely too much on this. Information to prove copying may not be available; the copying may have been innocent in intent; and in any case, the fact of copying does not suffice to establish passing off: this could be outweighed by other factors, such as active efforts by the defendant to differentiate its goods in the market place. This is the more likely if the branding is only marginally distinctive. If so, a limited effort at differentiation such as the addition of a distinctive trade name, may be enough to communicate that the goods are the defendant's own. Consequently, a comprehensive assessment is needed.

What does it take to be distinctive?

The term distinctiveness is used in respect of passing off to indicate what significance the buying public places upon a sign or combination of elements such as name and packaging.

A sign is distinctive if, in the minds of the public, it indicates the trade source of the goods or services. If the public do not regard it in this sense but only as a type of goods, for instance, then even if it is eccentric and remarkable, it is not distinctive. The problem arises in relation to products which have themselves an aesthetic function (clothing, decorative household objects and furnishings) or potentially a technical one (the shape and colouring of pharmaceutical products and medical devices). So for instance in *Glaxo Wellcome UK Ltd (t/a Allen & Hanburys) v Sandoz Ltd and Vectura (*[2019] EWHC 2545 (Ch)) the court rejected Glaxo's claim that the colour purple on an asthma inhaler indicated who manufactured it. Both patients and health care professionals understood the use of purple as the colour for an inhaler to indicate that it contained salmeterol as the active ingredient – an important indicator, especially for patients needing several different inhalers, but not one linked to the goodwill of Glaxo's business.

Even a sign which is apparently descriptive of the goods or services in question may with time and use become associated in the public's mind with a particular producer, thus acquiring distinctiveness. So there is no such thing as a hopelessly non-distinctive sign for passing off. But the more descriptive or innocuous a sign is, the heavier the evidential burden the branded business will bear in attempting to convince a court that it was, in practice, distinctive. It will be relatively easy to argue for the defence that the public saw the sign as a description of the type of goods, and that minor differences in the rival's sign for its own products are sufficient to enable customers to discriminate between them. It is also a defence, as for registered trade mark infringement claims, to show that the sign has become generic for the category of goods it is used for. No matter how novel a mark may be to start with, if in time it becomes so successful that the public adopt it as the name for the kind of goods – as Biro became for ballpoint pens or Hoover for vacuum cleaners – then it no longer distinguishes the branded goods to the exclusion of others.

A specific question arises where the branded business has for any reason enjoyed a monopoly on sales of the goods or services in question, whether through ownership of a patent or an exclusive licence of some kind. At the expiry of the monopoly it is likely that the market will recognise the brand name which has been used, but unless the brand is inherently distinctive the name of the product may simply be taken as the name for the type of product, especially if it is at all descriptive (*British Vacuum Cleaner Co Ltd v New Vacuum Cleaner Co Ltd* [1907] 2 Ch. 312). A monopoly in a particular get-up, however, does not suffer the same drawback: 30 years of being the only seller of lemon juice in yellow plastic lemons was sufficient to enable Reckitt & Colman Ltd to demonstrate distinctiveness of what might otherwise have been a descriptive sign, since other manufacturers had used a variety of different bottles for the juice (*Reckitt & Colman Ltd v Borden* [1990] 1 All ER 873).

As this discussion shows, there is no rule of thumb which can reliably be used in all circumstances to determine whether or not a sign in use has become distinctive. The more novel a name and the less connected with the type of goods or services, the easier it will be to show distinctiveness. Completely invented words such as Kodak, or words used completely out of their natural context (Penguin for chocolate biscuits), will more easily be seen as distinctive than more descriptive words, and it is impossible for a rival trader to use them without some reference to the branded business. Some more descriptive signs may become distinctive rapidly, as when launched following intensive prior publicity;

others may be in use but in a low-key fashion for several years before starting to achieve recognition in the relevant markets. It is a question of fact in every case. But the less unique the sign itself is, the higher the level of recognition it will be necessary to show in order to establish that a rival trader's sign which, though similar, is different in some respects will still cause the relevant public to be deceived.

To take a hypothetical example, a car dealer called Motorways will struggle to establish passing off by a rival dealer calling itself Motorway Sports: both names are intrinsically somewhat descriptive of a business dealing in cars. If the rival business opens when Motorways has been trading only for a year, few potential customers will yet have come to recognise its name at all and very few are likely to make any sort of assumption as to an association between the businesses. Clear, detailed evidence will be needed if Motorways is to show that its profile during its brief existence has been enough to make a somewhat descriptive name distinctive enough with customers for a risk of deception to arise. But if Motorways has been established and trading on the same site for 50 years, with many repeat customers and a high level of local recognition, then it may well be distinctive enough that a new business opening as Motorway Sports could be taken by some locals to be a new branch of the same business, possibly one focussing on sports models. The original Motorways will still, however, need to demonstrate that this has happened or is likely to, by reference to its volume of sales, spend on advertising and other publicity activities over the years, and relying on any comments or questions made by customers about the new business.

Losing distinctiveness

A business which ceases trading will, sooner or later, be forgotten and any distinctiveness which its branding may have acquired will be lost. How long this takes depends, as usual, upon the facts: how inherently distinctive or otherwise the sign was; how well known the business was when it stopped trading; what other brands are in the market for the same goods and how similar their brands are to that of the defunct business. It may be months or, as in the Barnsley Brewery case mentioned in Chapter 3 above, many years.

But distinctiveness can also be lost despite the business continuing to trade. For instance, if rivals use very similar signs for a prolonged period the distinctiveness of the original brand will be eroded as customers come to use other means to differentiate between sellers. This will not be the case, of course, if customers do not realise that the goods do not all come from the branded business: highly successful passing off, ironically, will not affect the branded business' rights (*AB Manus v J Fullwood & Bland Ltd* (1949) 66 RPC 71, CA).

The same effect may arise if the brand is widely licensed to others without close control of the uses licensees make of it.

What kind of signs can be relied upon?

It is true, though not very helpful, to say that any feature of a product or its marketing identifiers can either individually or collectively come to be recognised as a sign that the goods originate from one particular business. Names and any other kind of words, particularly invented ones, for either a product or the business which sells it are the commonest. Logos of all kinds from the simplest (such as the Nike 'swoosh' (which is, however, registered as a trade mark)) to the most complex combinations of pictures, special calligraphy and geometrical devices are widely used and relied upon. Combinations of colours used on lettering, labels or packaging may be recognisable and evocative of a trade source. In principle even the layout of features of packaging; shapes of products or packaging (such as distinctive bottles); letters, numerals and potentially slogans could be distinctive of a business.

In practice the courts have been reluctant to accept the shape of goods as a brand, and slogans may be understood by customers merely as persuasion or description rather than branding as such. For instance, in *McCain International Ltd v Country Fair Foods Ltd* ([1981] RPC 69CA) the phrase Oven Chips was held not to be recognised as distinctive of McCain, even though they had invented and publicised both the product and the name for it. Customers thought it was simply the appropriate term for chips which are cooked not in a deep fat fryer but in an oven. Similarly, customers rarely recognise a product purely based upon the look of the goods or the packaging. Such features may constitute part of an overall brand alongside a name or logo, but will rarely be the sole or definitive component. Features of the goods themselves may well be recognised, but buyers are more likely to note them for their functional or aesthetic importance rather than as an indicator of source. An exception to this is where goods are supplied in re-usable containers which are themselves recognisable as the branded business'. If a rival business accepts the empties and refills them without making sufficient effort to ensure that buyers know the current contents are not those of the original seller, this can be passing off (*Sodastream v Thorn Cascade Co* [1982] RP 459). It will not, however, be actionable if the service is the refilling of empty containers provided by the end customer and returned full to the same customer, even if prohibited by the original supplier of the containers to the customer, since there is then no representation made by the refiller (*New Zealand Industrial Gases v Oxyman* (1992) 24 IPR 161).

Product get-up can be relied upon other than components of it which are common to the trade, meaning in general use. The fact that one or another trader is using one or another aspect of packaging which are the same as the branded product does not make those aspects common to the trade. And even if the branded product's packaging includes some aspects which are common to the trade, or which it has itself adopted from an earlier user, the get-up taken as a whole may still be distinctive of the brand. Provided that a rival has adopted that distinctive collection, or those components of it which render it distinctive, then it may amount to a misrepresentation of origin.

Conversely, however, totally unique get-up may not be distinctive, if customers do not view it as an indicator of trade origin. This may be because the brand name is so recognisable that customers pay no attention to the get-up, or because it is seen as functional or for other reasons. For instance, the colour of packaging may be connected with the nature of the goods – as with the yellow colour for the plastic lemons in the *Jif Lemon* case (*Reckitt & Colman v Borden* [1990] 1 All ER 873). Or if a manufacturer uses different colours, or different combinations, for different goods, customers may see the colour as denoting which type or quality of goods the package contains, rather than their origin (*Rizla v Bryant & May* [1986] RPC 389). As with most aspects of passing off claims, the specific product, market and common practice will need to be considered in order to assess how distinctive a colour or combination are, in any particular dispute.

Personal names and place names can come to be distinctive of a particular business, whether or not the name is that of the person or the place in which they trade. Choice of a foreign name is as good a way as any of coming up with a brand name which is not descriptive of the product. A business called Timbuktu selling lighting products or computer software would be highly distinctive. Geographical designations for goods, such as champagne or Swiss chocolate, are a different category, discussed in chapters 8, 3 (standing of consortia to bring claims) and 5 (customers' understanding of designation).

It is possible in theory for the appearance of business premises – a shop front, decoration and layout – to form the basis for a claim of passing off, but no such claim has yet succeeded in the UK although one has in Canada (*Mr Submarine v Voultsos* (1977) 36 CPR (2d) 270) where the principles are very similar.

Now that much browsing and some purchasing is done online, video clips, memes of all kinds (aural and visual) and animations can equally be indicative of a particular business. What matters is that the sign, whatever it is, is used to identify the seller's goods or services and is understood as such by prospective customers.

Nicknames and abbreviations

A business can rely upon recognition of a sign which it has not itself chosen but which has been adopted by its customers, such as an abbreviation or alternative form of name. The manufacturer of the well-known drinks flavouring Angostura Bitters, for instance, had actually chosen the name Aromatic Bitters for its product, which was made in a town called Angostura. The public, and subsequently a rival business, adopted the name Angostura Bitters for the product and the original manufacturer was able to prevent its rival from using that name (*Siegert v Findlater* (1878) 7 ChD 801). The public may similarly interfere with the defendant's chosen sign: in the dispute over the famous Penguin biscuit, when Asda launched their own version as the ASDA Puffin, the evidence showed that consumers ignored the store name to focus only on the black-and-white bird designation, so increasing the likelihood of it being mistaken for the original Penguin (*United Biscuits (UK) Ltd v Asda Stores Ltd* [1997] RPC 513).

Uniqueness

It is not necessary for the sign to be unique to the claimant if the use of similar signs by others has not been such as to cause any confusion among customers as to whose goods are whose, while the defendant's use is of such a kind (*Parker & Son (Reading) v Parker* [1965] RPC 323). Indeed, if there is a chance that several businesses' customers could be confused by the new enterprise's branding, they may each have a claim in passing off for their own goodwill. But the existence in the market of other substantial businesses using the same or a very similar sign for the same or related goods or services will inevitably make it harder to show that the sign is sufficiently distinctive of the branded business. Thus, Imperial Tobacco, the makers of the John Player brand of cigarettes, failed when claiming passing off against another cigarette maker for using a pure black pack like the John Player Special brand as the black pack alone was not distinctive of their brand (*Imperial Group plc v Philip Morris Ltd* [1984] RPC 293).

The existence of a far more famous brand using the same sign can, however, complicate a claim even if it is being used in a wholly unrelated field. The problem here is that consumers faced with either of two smaller businesses using the same sign in a different market may think first of the large, well-known brand instead. As a result the second-comer's misrepresentation, if any, is of association with that third company (*Rolls Razor v Rolls Lighters* (1949) 66 RPC 299, CA). Similarly, a brand with a potential geographical connotation may not be distinctive of a particular enterprise if consumers understand the brand to relate to the location or origin of the business instead.

Assessing distinctiveness and deception

Given that so many aspects of a product and how it is sold may go to make up the brand recognition among customers, the assessment of what factors contribute to that distinctiveness must be wide-ranging. Indeed, it is one of the strengths of the tort that the branded business need not define in advance what the branding consists in, instead choosing those features which the rival has seen fit to copy, in order to emphasise the importance of the similarities.

The idea of the brand

This works particularly well if the brand consists of a readily identifiable idea. Thus, United Biscuits succeeded in claiming passing off against Asda despite failing in its trade mark infringement claim: the name of the copycat biscuit, Puffin, was too different from the original Penguin to infringe the registration. But the facts that

- both names represent small black and white seabirds,
- neither name has anything to do with chocolate biscuits, and
- the two products were packaged similarly, in packs of 6 in a plastic film package

enabled the court to conclude consumers might be deceived (*United Biscuits (UK) Ltd v Asda Stores Ltd* [1997] RPC 513). Had Asda chosen to sell the same biscuits as Eagle or Robin, the claim would have had much less chance of success.

Price

The likelihood of deception will also depend upon the type of goods and so the care customers may be assumed to take in choosing a particular product. Shoppers buying processed cheese are unlikely to consider each packet very carefully. Indeed, some may not even care what cheese they get, in which case they are not the category of customers to consider in this exercise, since they are never deceived (*Schweppes Ltd v Gibbens* (1905) 22 RPC 601). But when they buy premium whisky or a robot lawnmower they will take a closer look.

Even buyers of very expensive goods may, however, have special characteristics which render them at risk of deception. For instance, the jeweller Asprey & Garrards has many foreign customers who, though rich, may have limited knowledge of English or London and thus potentially be confused by coming across another shop calling itself Asprey (*Asprey & Garrard Ltd V WRA (Guns) Ltd and Asprey* [2001] EWCA Civ 499).

How many are deceived

It is not necessary for all of the relevant public to be likely to be deceived, provided that a substantial proportion may be. But once again, the degree of inherent distinctiveness of the sign is a factor here: a whimsical and invented brand will be protected at a relatively low proportion of customers recognising it, whereas an innocuous or somewhat descriptive brand will need to show a higher proportion. This is exacerbated by the fact that customers for many kinds of goods may remember the specific signs of a brand only imperfectly, so that a strict side-by-side comparison of the brand with the rival trader's goods is not always fair to the brand.

The issue has to be assessed by considering ordinary buyers of the goods concerned, neither excessively cautious nor excessively careless (the famous 'moron in a hurry' who may miss even substantial differences when buying their morning newspaper). If the goods are sold to other traders rather than the general public, then the buyers can be assumed to be more knowledgeable and careful in their choices.

Sales channel

The sales channel is also important. Surfing online for goods in peace and quiet is quite different from buying from a market stall with a queue behind one, but the online buyer depends on the photographs displayed of the product rather than being able to examine them themselves. If the buyer is deceived, their being able to return the goods on opening the package is no defence, since this entails substantial inconvenience and only a few buyers will ever bother. Goods bought over the counter depend on one party being able to pronounce and the other able to hear the product name, whereas the packaging may only be seen by the customer after the purchase. More exclusive products may only be accessible through speaking to a sales assistant – who may either assist the customer to work out exactly what they want or, if so instructed or incentivised, actively divert the customer to a rival product. Each of these issues will need to be considered.

Two sides of a coin

It is important to bear in mind throughout this exercise that distinctiveness and deceptiveness are two sides of the same coin. Where a sign is only mildly distinctive, because somewhat descriptive for instance, then a rival trader may use a sign which is only slightly different without necessarily raising a risk of deception of customers. Laudatory terms suffer the same problem: calling a product Tasty Beans will not differentiate it very well so a rival trader might be able to sell Tangy Beans in similar packaging – all beans are sold in standard sized tins - without causing any deception.

If the brand is highly distinctive, then a rival trader will need either to use a completely unrelated sign, or if for some reason it chooses to use a similar or related sign it must add sufficient distinguishing features to counteract the inherent risk of deception (whether intentional or not). At the bottom end of the scale, a rival trader has the right to use a descriptive term *in order to describe its products or services*, even if the term is being used by another as a brand. The branded business cannot object purely to its use at all. Clearly, an issue immediately arises as to whether the rival is also to some extent using the term in the brand or trade mark sense, and if so to what extent. But if an enterprise chooses to use even a partially descriptive term as its brand, then it must accept that there will always be some ambiguity as to the term's function and an on-going risk that other traders will be permitted to use it as well, using only limited differentiation to avoid making a misrepresentation.

A particular form of this issue concerns newly invented products, epitomised by the claim brought over the use of the word Linoleum. The original inventor of the substance linoleum necessarily had to invent a name for the product and made up the word Linoleum for that purpose. Sales were initially protected by a patent over the making of the substance. But when the patent expired, other traders became entitled to make and sell the substance. A claim that they were passing it off by calling it linoleum failed, because there was no other name by which they could have called it. If the inventor had wanted to protect it as a brand, it would have needed not only to name the new substance but also to come up with a separate trade name for it, so that new entrants into the market would have had to create their own goodwill in dealing with it under their own trade names (*Linoleum Manufacturing Co v Nairn* (1878) 7 ChD 834).

Distinctiveness online

The use of a domain name which incorporates a brand name associated with another business is capable of amounting to passing off provided that when a user actually visits the site the content is presented in a way which at least maintains the misrepresentation of possible association with the brand. The law here is very much in an early stage of development. In the early days of the internet the courts were persuaded that simply registering a domain name using another's brand could constitute passing off (*British Telecommunications plc v One in a Million Ltd* [1999] 1 WLR 903), but both users and courts have become far more sophisticated. Today it is uncertain that even if the site is actually trading the use of a domain name which incorporated or referenced another's brand would, alone, be sufficient to establish the necessary misrepresentation if, when a customer is actually on the rival site, it is made clear that the goods or services offered are not those of the branded business (*Media Agency Group Ltd v Space Media Agency Ltd* [2019] EWCA Civ 712). It would otherwise be inconsistent with the former offline approach that provided the misrepresentation, if any, has been dissipated by the point of purchase there is no passing off. However, the current more restrictive approach in registered trade mark law, that initial interest confusion is sufficient to constitute infringement, has been held to be arguable as passing off online (*Och-Ziff Management v OCH Capital* [2010] EWHC 2599 (Ch)) but not yet considered by the higher courts. The judge who decided that case, Arnold J, has since been appointed to the Court of Appeal.

Indeed, now that most internet searching is done through search engines rather than by guessing the name of the appropriate site, many users may not actually notice the name of the site their search engine proposes. This raises the question of use of brands as metatags, the sign-posts embedded in a site's code for the use of search engines. Use of a trade mark as a metatag to cause adverts for a rival business' site to be displayed when a user typed the Interflora trade mark was litigated extensively in *Interflora Inc and another v Marks and Spencer plc* ([2014] EWCA Civ 1403, [2014] All ER (D) 55). Passing off was not in issue in that dispute as customers never see the metatags on a site, they are for the use of the computer only. However, the conclusion – that the metatags giving rise to the advertisements do not constitute trade mark infringement provided that the advertisements displayed to users do not themselves include the Interflora mark – are equally applicable in principle to unregistered brands. A computer which chooses an advertisement to present based upon code invisible to the user cannot be said to be deceived; and if the user is not then deceived by the advertisement itself, then there cannot be said to have been any effective misrepresentation.

Ultimately, unless the use of the brand online can be shown to be a misrepresentation which diverts trade significantly away from the branded business, then its use either as a domain name or metatag is unlikely to constitute passing off. A branded business would still need to establish that the false belief that the two businesses are associated is damaging to the goodwill or that it eroded the distinctiveness of the brand (*Moroccanoil Israel Limited v Aldi Stores Limited* [2014] EWHC 1686).

CHAPTER EIGHT
EXPANDING THE BOUNDARIES: REVERSE PASSING OFF AND OTHER ACTIONABLE MISREPRESENTATIONS

The previous two chapters have dealt in depth with the ramifications of the commonest form of passing off, namely some kind of representation that the defendant's goods or services are those of the branded business. But passing off is not limited to that form of misrepresentation. It is a flexible tort, and many other means of attempting to benefit from a rival's goodwill will also be actionable. This chapter deals in some of those other forms of representation.

Reverse passing off

The underlying objection to passing off is that one trader takes advantage of customers and a rival business by appropriating a reputation which actually attaches to the other trader. The name reverse or inverse passing off is given to the situation where the unscrupulous trader claims that the reputable trader's goods or services are, in fact his own i.e. that the good reputation of the reputable trader has been built on goods or services devised or supplied by the unscrupulous one.

In the leading case of *Bristol Conservatories v Conservatories Custom Built* ([1989] RPC 455, CA) the defendant took on a salesman formerly employed by the claimant. The salesman had kept a book of photographs of the claimant's conservatories and thereafter used these to promote the new business, telling prospective customers that these were the new company's conservatories. This was held to be an actionable misrepresentation even though the prospective customers knew nothing of the claimant's business at all; it was enough that the claimant's expertise and reputation (implied by the existence of numerous prior projects) were being appropriated. Copying another trader's catalogue and samples and using them to promote rival (and inferior) goods is a similar form of passing off (*Masson, Seeley & Co Ltd v Embossotype Manufacturing Ltd* (1924) 41 RPC 160).

Earlier cases dealt with matters such as a trader displaying as its own testimonials, reviews (*Samuelson v Producers Distributing Co* (1931) 48 RPC 580 CA) or prizes (*National Starch Manufacturing Co v Munn's Patent Maienza and Starch Co* [1894] AC275) which had in fact been won by the branded business' owner.

The nineteenth century also saw a range of cases in which the passing off took the form of a false claim that the goods were 'the original' or patent protected, when in fact it was another trader's goods to which the patent applied (*Spalding (AG) & Bros v AW Gamage Ltd* (1915) 32 RPC 273). However, the current law provides a more effective remedy for such misrepresentations by making it a criminal offence for a person to falsely represent that anything disposed of by him for value is a patented product (s110(1) Patents Act 1977). The punishment is a fine at level 3 on the standard scale.

Although the term reverse passing off is used, the cause of action remains passing off: there has been no new tort introduced. It is important to recognise that the courts have not been enthusiastic, in the physical world at least, to expand the scope of passing off beyond such clearly analogous circumstances to cover other commercial disputes which, for whatever reason, do not constitute trade mark infringement. The evolving law of passing off online, where new and unfamiliar opportunities for misleading customers abound, may prove more generous.

The new business is connected to the branded business

If a business presents itself to potential customers as in some way a part of, associated with or backed by a brand originator, such that the brand originator has a degree of responsibility for the quality of the new business' goods or services, then that misrepresentation is sufficient to found a claim in passing off (*Harrods Ltd v Harrodian School Ltd* [1996] RPC 697, CA). It is not necessary for the misrepresentation to allege any specific connection, since the public at large is unlikely to understand the various forms of business connection which exist. If belief in a connection is created, and it is such that damage is likely to be caused as a result, the misrepresentation is established and there is no additional advantage in proving that a particular relationship was being implied. A representation that the new business has taken over that of the brand, for instance because the latter has gone out of business, is actionable to the same extent as a mere suggestion that the new business is a separate branch of the branded business, a different company within the same group, or an agent of or licensed or approved by it. A representation that the business is a member of a particular association or certified or approved by it is likewise actionable, if damage can be shown (as discussed in Chapter 3).

A particular form of misrepresentation may be made by a business which is, in fact, a representative or licensee of the brand, but which offers goods of its own without making plain that they are *not* those of the branded business. The implicit representation that the goods are the branded business' is actionable (*International Scientific Communications Inc v Pattison* [1979] FSR 429).

A misrepresentation that a business is licensed by the branded business when in fact any such licence has been terminated, or is limited to another class of goods or services, will be actionable (*Dawnay Day & Co Ltd v Cantor Fitzgerald International* [2000] RPC 669).

A statement that the business' goods are similar to, or suitable as substitutes for, the branded products are not necessarily misrepresentations at all provided that they are not such as to lead customers to believe there is any association between the two suppliers. Nor does a statement that the branded business has sponsored or supported the new business necessarily imply that it stands behind the new business in the way that an owner, associate company or licensor might do (*Harrods Ltd v Harrodian School Ltd* [1996] RPC 697, CA).

Personality merchandising and endorsement

Merchandising both in relation to fictitious characters and celebrities is a powerful promotional tool for memorabilia of all kinds, which may in themselves be of variable quality. Character merchandising encompasses a range of activities which share the common feature that they involve the licensing of the names or likenesses of famous characters, whether real or fictional. For example, there may be a relatively simple licence in place, possibly a licence of copyright material. Endorsement, on the other hand, describes one particular kind of relationship between the characters (or their creators) and the goods which bear their names or likenesses, and it implies authorisation and approval. Celebrities may be paid for endorsing products, in the hope that "the lustre of a famous personality, if attached to their goods or services, will enhance the attractiveness of those goods or services to their target market" (*Irvine v Talksport Ltd* [2002] EWHC 367 (Ch)). The new profession of internet influencers take the market for endorsement to the limit at which it shades into pure advertising, in that the influencers' expertise may be little more than how to appear to greatest advantage in photographs and videos. Nevertheless, successful influencers do attract substantial followings and their endorsements have in recent years been sought after by advertisers for all kinds of products.

The right to object to one's name or likeness being used for an apparent endorsement without consent may seem to be a form of image or publicity right, but English law does not recognise any such right. Instead, the classic passing off analysis must be applied: is there a misrepresentation, and is it likely to damage the celebrity's goodwill in their commercial capacity? Accordingly, an individual who has no commercial profile will struggle to prevent the use of their image in an apparent endorsement unless data privacy law can be called in aid.

Indeed, even the extremely famous cannot assume that simply because their name or image appears upon a consumable commercial item, the public will assume that it has in some way been endorsed by them. The Estate of Elvis Presley failed to register a trade mark Elvis Presley in respect of toiletries, on the ground it was simply not distinctive: members of the public purchased Elvis Presley merchandise not because it came from a particular source, but because it carried the name or image of Elvis Presley (*Elvis Presley Trade Marks* [1999] RPC 567). Where, however, the circumstances indicate that a substantial proportion of buyers will assume such an endorsement is being made, and will be more likely to buy the goods because of it, then unauthorised use of a name or image may be actionable. Thus when Rihanna sued TopShop for sale of a T-shirt bearing a photograph of her taken during the making of a video for a recent single, she succeeded because she was able to show that:

- fans were more likely to buy the shirt in the belief that she, a style icon as much as a singer, had endorsed it, and
- such a belief was likely in view of
    - the posed-looking nature of the photograph and
    - her previous association with promotions for TopShop as well as more prestigious brands such as Gucci (*Robyn Rihanna Fenty & Ots v Arcadia Group Brands Ltd & Anr* [2015] EWCA Civ 3).

The Court of Appeal did, however, state that even so the case was a borderline one.

Rihanna's case illustrates the difficulty that a real person with a strong reputation and significant business interests may have in claiming passing off by use of a name or image. The same difficulty applies where the activity concerned is character merchandising: it will be necessary to show that the relevant public believes that any product bearing the relevant name or image must be manufactured under a licence including quality control provisions such that buyers are likely to prefer licensed or authorised goods to unauthorised ones (*Taverner Routledge Ltd v Trexapalm Ltd* [1975] FSR 479).

Substitution and switch selling

Where a customer requests the branded goods and is sold another product, this will amount to passing off unless the customer knowingly and voluntarily accepts the alternative. A customer who fails to notice has been deceived, even if a more alert customer might have realised what has happened. Customers are also entitled to assume that a request has been properly fulfilled, not to treat all businesses with suspicion.

Substitution in a transaction face to face with the customer is highly likely to be passing off because an opportunity to explain the substitution existed and was not taken. With the increase in remote transacting, the opportunity to explain may be limited or non-existent. But it is no defence to say that a customer could tell the difference when they received the goods – indeed, may even have been expressly informed at that point - and, not having returned them, must have been happy with the substitution. Returning goods, especially if the product does actually work, is a hassle many customers will not undertake; and a sale has still been lost for the brand (*Purefoy Engineering Ltd v Sykes* (1954) 72 RPC 89). If, however, the context of the sale indicates that the customer was happier to accept substitute goods than none, and the branded goods were not available, then this may not constitute a misrepresentation.

Switch selling is an even more questionable practice, where the business advertises or offers the original goods but then supplies others, either without explanation or after a sales pitch in their favour. If the latter, then it is more problematic to argue a claim in passing off since at the time of the purchase the customer knows it is not getting the original goods it sought. Nonetheless, a misrepresentation has been made which may have been instrumental in achieving the sale and so causing damage. The success of a claim is likely to depend upon demonstrating that customers have a preference for the branded goods and so would not have approached this seller if they knew that the branded product was not on offer. If, on the contrary, customers ordinarily buy any substitutable product then the case is more one of the brand having become a shorthand for the type of goods, and passing off will be difficult to establish.

Designations of origin or type of goods

There have been a number of cases concerning goods protected by a geographical designation of origin, since such designations indicate some specific characteristic of the goods concerned and a definite connection with a place. As a result, they can be relied upon as distinctive of a product by not just one but any business which trades in goods legitimately entitled to the designation. The use of the designation is normally managed by a consortium or trade association; businesses which make a product not meeting the appropriate specification are not entitled to use the designation even if they manufacture in the same geographical area. In such cases, the misrepresentation made by a business improperly calling its product champagne (*Taittinger SA v Allbev Ltd* [1994] All ER 75), or Harris Tweed (*Argyllshire Weavers Ltd v A Macaulay Tweeds Ltd* [1964] RPC 477) is not that its goods are those of a particular brand, but that they have the characteristics of the goods properly so-called, whether that be the geographical source, ingredients or means of production (hand-weaving, in the case of Harris tweed). As the cases cited here show, the courts will permit one or more of the businesses which are properly entitled to the designation to bring a passing off claim, effectively on behalf of all but recovering damages only insofar as its own trade has been affected.

The principle was expanded in the *Advocaat* case (*Erwin Warnink v Townend* [1979] All ER 927) to cover any well-defined product regardless of a particular geographical association. Advocaat originated as a drink in the Netherlands, where it is made by a number of different producers, but always with brandy (among other ingredients). The defendant Townend offered a similar drink but made with a form of sherry. The House of Lords agreed with Warnink that to offer this as Advocaat did misrepresent in a way that damaged its goodwill and was accordingly passing off.

Denial of existence and denigration

If a trader feels unable to divert trade by any other means, they may occasionally be reduced to denying that the branded business still exists or still trades in the relevant field. This may be passing off if the impression created is that the rival trader is the successor in business (*Worsley v Cooper* [1939] 1All ER 290), but otherwise would be actionable, if at all, as injurious falsehood (for which proof of ill intent is necessary).

Likewise, statements that the branded goods are unsuitable or inferior are, if false, injurious falsehoods; but they are less likely to be actionable as passing off since the maker of the statements is not taking any benefit from the branded business' goodwill. Assertions that the branded goods are themselves passing off or trade mark infringements in some way may be disparaging through the imputation that the branded business is a counterfeiter or otherwise a less than honest trader, but once again do not attempt to attract to the maker any advantage from the branded business' goodwill and so are not actionable as passing off. If taken far enough, disparaging comments may be actionable as defamatory, but in order to be so it must be shown that anyone (other than the offended target) takes them seriously (*British Airways plc v Ryanair Ltd* [2001] FSR 32).

False advertising

Making false statements without reference to any other trader or their goods is unlikely to be actionable either as passing off or injurious falsehood. For instance, a claim brought by a dental supplies firm objecting to a rival making false assertions as to the efficacy of a particular dental disinfectant was rejected on both counts (*Schulke & Mayr UK Ltd v Alkapharm UK Ltd* [1999] FSR 161) for lack of connection to the claimant: neither business' product had the quality claimed. If, on the other hand the claimant's disinfectant had had the effectiveness claimed, while the defendant's did not, then it may have been possible to infer that the defendant was making an implicit comparison with the claimant, which may have been passing off (in the inverse form). But without such connection, the false statements were merely false advertising and so fell within the remit of the Advertising Standards Authority or Trading Standards functions of local authorities.

CHAPTER NINE
DEFENCES

From the brand originator's point of view there is rarely any such thing as a clear-cut, simple claim in passing off. Proving the existence of goodwill, the nature and impact of the rival's misrepresentation are all potentially fraught with difficulties. Accordingly, attack is the best form of defence: the principal line of defence of any trader accused of passing off is often simply putting the claimant to strict proof on each of the core issues.

A number of other arguments have of course been developed over the years, some with greater chances of success than others.

Own name

Individual traders, though not companies, may be entitled to use their own names in trade if the use is in good faith despite the use potentially otherwise amounting to a misrepresentation. The use must be the full name, not a surname alone or any nickname or abbreviation, and it must be the name of the business, not the name of goods or services. Further, the trader must do nothing more, which might cause confusion with the branded business, other than use their own name (*Parker-Knoll Ltd v Knoll International Ltd* [1962] RPC 265).

These restrictions demonstrate that the courts are generally reluctant to allow an individual to continue trading under a name if all of the requirements of misrepresentation and damage to another's goodwill have been made out against them. Indeed, if the risk of confusion is apparent even before the business is set up, it might be considered less than perfect good faith to choose to trade under the name rather than to select another, and recent decisions have tended not to accept the defence for that reason. Nevertheless, if a trader using their own name were to take suitable measures to reduce the risk of confusion then, in principle, the defence could still be invoked (*Asprey & Garrard Ltd v WRA (Gins) Ltd and Asprey* [2001] EWCA 1499).

Innocence

Since the trader's intentions in making the statement which is found to be a misrepresentation is irrelevant, it follows that a plea of innocent intent is no defence to a claim in passing off. It may in the past have had some bearing upon the availability to a successful claimant of the equitable remedy of an account of profits but this question has not been considered in recent cases. In any event, the objective in the majority of passing off claims is to obtain an injunction to prevent repetition of the misrepresentation, and this certainly remains available no matter how innocently the misrepresentation may initially have been made.

Concurrent or earlier rights

The contraction of distance as a bar to trading has meant that businesses which a century ago might never have heard of each other may now come into direct competition. Alternatively, a business may be sold or split off from a group so that more than one trader exists with a claim to use the name of the original group (though this issue ought, of course, to have been foreseen and addressed in the agreement by which the separation took place).

In either situation, a trader which has for some time and honestly been using a particular name is likely to be aggrieved if faced with a claim that continuing use will amount to passing itself off as another trader. If, for instance, the name used by a small local business is adopted by a party with deep pockets and a ferocious advertising budget, the effect may after a while be that customers other than the established customer base come to imagine that the smaller business is in some way an offshoot of or, worse, copier of the larger. Nevertheless, the courts will not injunct a trader from continuing such long established and honest use (*Pitman Training v Nominet UK and Pearson* [1997] EWHC Ch 367).

The defence is, however, limited to the trade which has already been established under that name: the trader cannot later expand under the same name into different fields (*Reed Executive plc v Reed Business Information Ltd* [2002] EWHC 1015) or territories (*Cavendish House v Cavendish-Woodhouse* [1970] RPC 234) which the rival business already occupies.

It follows that a business which is well established in another country is not thereby entitled to expand under the same name into the UK if traders in the UK are already using the same name on goods (*Island Trading Company v Anchor Brewing Company* [1989] RPC 287). If, however, the foreign business' reputation in the UK is sufficient to negate any risk of deception of UK consumers then the brand may already have ceased to be distinctive of its UK user, and there may be no misrepresentation through the foreign business commencing to use it in the UK. The increasing penetration of internet access among consumers may bring about more such instances in the future, as customers are exposed to publicity about foreign companies frequently without it being made apparent where, geographically, the business is located.

Conversely, as discussed in Chapter 3, existence of a reputation in the UK based solely on established trade abroad is not sufficient to constitute the UK goodwill needed for a passing off claim (*Starbucks (HK) Ltd v BSkyB Group* [2015] UKSC 31).

Delay, acquiescence and estoppel

Delay as such is not a defence to a claim in passing off, although it may weaken it by enabling the rival trader to establish recognition and so dilute the distinctiveness of the brand as regards the original user's business.

Where the delay occurs despite full knowledge of the rival's activities, however, then eventually such acquiescence in the rival's activities may provide a defence, although something more than simply ignoring the activity is required. The essence of acquiescence or estoppel as an equitable defence is that the rival relies on some action, representation or default of the brand originator as giving it the right to make use of the brand, and alters its position as a result. It is not impossible for simple failure to act to constitute acquiescence, but the failure must amount to standing by "in such a manner as really to induce the person committing the act, and who might otherwise have abstained from it, to believe that he assents to its being committed; a person so standing by cannot afterwards be heard to complain of the act. In that sense the doctrine of acquiescence may be defined as quiescence under such circumstances that assent may be reasonably inferred from it, and is no more than an instance of the law of estoppel by words or conduct" (Halsbury's Laws of England). In an extreme case, *Vine Products Limited v MacKenzie & Co Limited* ([1969] RPC 1), British sherry makers had been allowed by Spanish sherry distributors to build up goodwill in their brand 'British Sherry' over 100 years. The Court held that had the Spanish sherry distributors complained many years earlier, the use of the term might have amounted to passing off/unfair competition but because of the passage of time it would be inequitable to stop the British sherry makers from using the words. However, if the delay is of less than decades then some further action or omission (such as failure to respond to a letter notifying the branded business of the defendant's activities) will be needed.

When considering whether or not there has been an act of encouragement by the rights–holder, the seniority of the employee committing the act relied upon becomes relevant. A hint by an employee too junior to commit the company is unlikely to be sufficient (*Dyson Ltd v Qualtex (UK) Ltd* [2004] EWHC 2981).

The prejudice suffered by the defendant as a result of the branded business' conduct or inaction need not be financial, as long as it is "something substantial" (*Gillet v Holt* [2001] ChD 210).

Active assistance in setting a former subsidiary up as an independent UK business, upon nationalisation of the overseas parent company, was accepted by the Court of Appeal as sufficient to establish the defence for the UK business (although it in any event succeeded in defeating the passing off claim) (*Habib Bank Ltd v Habib Bank AG* [1981] 2 All ER 650).

As these defences are equitable, any conduct of the defendant which sullies its otherwise clean hands is likely to lead to the defence failing.

Restriction on competition and freedom of movement

So-called Euro-defences have become common in actions for infringement of intellectual property rights such as registered trade marks, and so might seem a potential source of defences in passing off actions as well. But on closer scrutiny, they are unlikely to have effect since the conflict between intellectual property rights and competition law arises due to the monopoly nature of intellectual property rights properly so called. Passing off is a cause of action which does not confer any such monopoly and so cannot give rise to any competition issues.

Similarly, the right under European Union law for traders to parallel import into the UK trade marked goods which have been released into free circulation by or with the approval of a trade mark owner, elsewhere in the European Union, is unlikely to affect the success or otherwise of a claim against passing those goods off once they are inside the UK. A passing off claim would be based on the importer misrepresenting the goods, say as a different grade to that which the branded business had marketed them as. Such a misrepresentation is equally unacceptable under EU law since it may harm consumers (*Rewe v Bundesmonopolverwaltung fur Branntwein* [1979] ECR 649, the *Cassis de Dijon* case).

The operation of the rules on freedom of movement may well change once the UK has left the EU, but if any new trade agreement makes any difference at all to the rules it will be more likely to enhance UK business' ability to object to parallel imports than to restrict it.

CHAPTER TEN
ENFORCEMENT

The principles of passing off each require proof, and the success or failure of any claim stands entirely on how credible the court finds the evidence underpinning it. Such evidence must be collected in a scrupulously court-worthy way, much of it before pleading the claim, and it is a costly exercise for an action with multiple contestable issues since there is unlikely to be any opportunity to add materiality once the defendant's evidence in refutation has been examined.

Courts and costs

As a common law tort, passing off does not come within the exclusive competence of the Patents Court of the Chancery Division ("PC") or the Intellectual Property Enterprise Court ("IPEC"). A claim suitable for the IPEC started in another court may well be transferred if either party requests it, however; and a claim started in the Chancery Division is likely to be heard by a Patents Court judge. Both courts have judges who are specialists in intellectual property, and IPEC publishes a Guide setting out their specialist rules and procedures, in addition to Part 63 of the Civil Procedure Rules and its Practice Direction. Parties will be expected to stick to these or justify any deviation.

The IPEC in particular is worth considering as a forum because of its costs regime. In the IPEC multi-track, litigants may claim an injunction and up to £500,000 in compensation but the costs which a winning party can claim from the losing party are capped at £50,000 and frequently less is recovered. The cap can be removed, but hardly ever is. Since the regime includes a cap for each individual stage of proceedings, there is no need to prepare and file a costs budget. In the small claims track the procedure is shorter and less formal but compensation is limited to £10,000. Generally, at the end of the case in this track the losing party will be required to pay little or none of the winning party's legal costs. There is thus even greater protection from an adverse order on costs if a party is not successful.

In the PC, the full range of remedies and compensation is available but the normal costs rules apply. Given the evidence-heavy nature of passing off litigation, this can lead to very expensive proceedings, even for the winning party. The PC judges will consider costs on an issue by issue basis and so a winning party which is found to have incurred costs unnecessarily on one or more issues may end up recovering a lesser proportion than the usual rule of thumb (which is 75-80% of the total actually spent) and occasionally considerably less.

Understandably, the IPEC route is popular, but popularity has had the unfortunate side-effect of slowing down the time taken to reach trial from an initial target of a few months so that a couple of years is now more likely. As of October 2019, there were to be district judges based in each of the six Business and Property Court centres out of London, namely Birmingham, Bristol, Cardiff, Leeds, Manchester and Newcastle, able to hear matters in the IPEC small claims track, which may assist.

Pre-action conduct

There is no pre-action protocol applicable to passing off cases, and so the general Practice Direction on Pre-Action Conduct applies: the claimant should write to the proposed defendant setting out the claim, and the defendant should respond within 14 days.

There is no statutory threats regime applicable to passing off cases (unlike claims for registered trade mark infringement) so the wording of the letter notifying the claim can be frank without risk of any pre-emptive action to restrain unjustified threats being filed. It is still important, however, to write in the knowledge that the letter will be placed before the judge at some point. Intemperate language and exaggerated claims can prejudice the court's view of a party. Further, a letter dealing with both passing off and registered trade mark infringement should be treated as subject to the threats regime; no amount of separation of language within one letter will persuade the court that a threat in passing off may not be read by the recipient as including a threat in registered trade mark infringement. Separate letters are less likely to incur this risk.

Pleading the claim

A claim in passing off must explain clearly and concisely the grounds on which the claim is based:

- who the claimant is, its trading status and goodwill;
- what form the misrepresentation alleged to have been made by the defendant takes – whether by use of a deceptive sign or through express statements or otherwise;
- where, when and to whom it has been or is being made; and
- the damage the claimant has suffered or expects to suffer as a result.

Of these, the misrepresentation is likely to be the most difficult, but it is made much simpler by the fact of not needing to allege any kind of intention on the defendant's part. The matter must be presented factually: this sign was used or this statement made. No reference to the defendant's objective in making the statement need be included, and especially no allegation of an intent to deceive or defraud. Pleading deception or fraud should only be done on the basis of clear, categorical evidence to that effect, not inference from the parties' past interactions or trading relationship. Such clear evidence is almost never available; whereas a plea of deception or fraud will inevitably lead to disputes over the appropriateness of the pleading and contests in court over disclosure which will add time, cost and bitterness to the dispute without increasing the likelihood of success in any material way. This can be difficult for a claimant outraged by another trader's conduct to appreciate.

Interim relief

The objective of a claim in passing off is normally to prevent the defendant from repeating the misrepresentation objected to, and an application for an interim injunction is the fastest way to achieve this. In practice a defendant may well agree to submit to an injunction pending trial provided that the claimant gives a cross-undertaking in damages to compensate it for the sales it will lose during that period, should it succeed in defeating the claim at trial. But if the defendant does not agree, the claimant will need to prove that an injunction is needed urgently, not just after trial. Essentially this requires evidence that the damage it will suffer during that period cannot be compensated in damages after trial, either because the damage – dilution of the distinctiveness of the brand, for instance – is unquantifiable or because the defendant will not have the resources to pay, or otherwise.

In principle, a claimant can also apply for a pre-action Search Order to obtain evidence in support of its claim. Part 25 of the Civil Procedure Rules and the Practice Direction to it apply, including the standard form of order. But given that the nature of the action presupposes misrepresentation being made to third parties, such orders are rarely needed.

Evidence

The evidence of the claimant's own goodwill should include trading accounts and marketing details for as long as available – although obviously for a very longstanding business, there is no need to go back decades. This evidence will generally not be contentious; and if the claimant is unwilling to disclose its current financial affairs to a distrusted competitor, it should be possible to agree a confidentiality arrangement limiting who has access to the information.

Likewise, damage to goodwill should require relatively limited evidence especially if the passing off has only recently begun so that neither loss of sales and customer confusion are likely to have become widespread. Clearly, if there is evidence of customer confusion this is very valuable. Social media records, records of customer conversations of all kinds and in particular any complaints which have reached the claimant concerning the defendant or its goods or services should be included in full.

Proving a misrepresentation

The area most likely to give rise to issues is, once again, the misrepresentation. In some cases this is straightforward: the product is available on the shelves bearing the brand or a close imitation of it, and samples can be bought. But if the defendant is selling to trade customers, or the misrepresentation is done through substitution or switch selling, it may be necessary to carry out a trap purchase in order to obtain a sample and evidence of the unscrupulous behaviour. This needs to be done in such a way that the individual buyer can give a witness statement and be cross-examined on how the purchase took place, without being accused of having tricked the defendant into an atypical transaction or leaving any room for doubt that the purchase was a normal one from the seller's perspective. Often a private investigator is used for such a transaction, but if the passing off has come to light by report from a supplier or customer common to both parties, their evidence (if they are willing to have their involvement disclosed) may be preferable, since it goes some way towards showing that other market participants perceive the defendant's conduct as a misrepresentation.

If evidence of consumer confusion or deception is not available, and the case is not one of outright copying of the brand on identical goods or services, then the claimant needs to find some means to persuade the court that confusion is likely. There are a number of possible approaches to this.

First, the claimant can give evidence on its own behalf to explain why it considers the defendant's conduct misrepresents something. This may edge into evidence of opinion but the claimant is, presumably, expert in its own market and has a right to explain to the court why it is bringing a claim. However, such evidence suffers from the obvious disadvantage of being one-sided and so the weight the court may give to it is likely to be limited.

Secondly, other traders or retailers may give evidence. This is valuable if the defendant is selling to the trade, but if the misrepresentation is instead being made directly to consumers then traders' opinions as to whether customers will be deceived is not necessarily very useful unless it comprises reports of actual customer confusion which they have encountered. The exception to this is where the goods are of a kind or in a market of which the court itself may have little or no experience (*Dalgety Spillers Foods Ltd v Food Brokers Ltd* [1994] FSR 504).

Thirdly, the claimant may seek to gather evidence from customers and potential customers themselves as to whether they have been or might be misled. Traditionally, this evidence was procured in the form of surveys carried out by market research organisations and presented in a dual form: with individual testimony from witnesses whose response to the survey indicated confusion, and with expert evidence from an expert in survey result interpretation. However, the courts have become increasingly hostile to survey evidence over the last decade with the effect that although not prohibited, an application for permission, based on a small pilot survey, will need to be made in order to carry out a survey. The applicant will need to justify: the questions to be asked; the survey protocol and locations; and the number of individuals to be surveyed. In recent cases, the courts have most frequently either refused permission to carry out a survey at all, or placed little or no weight on the evidence it produces. It is all too simple to criticise the questions which were asked as either misleading (or leading) themselves, or irrelevant as not being questions which consumers would normally consider. In *Interflora plc v Marks & Spencer plc* ([2012] EWCA Civ 1501) the Court of Appeal ruled that survey evidence would no longer be admitted in trade mark infringement cases without permission; and subsequently refused permission to adduce survey evidence in the first cases to come before it on the admissibility of survey evidence in a passing off case since that landmark judgment (*Zee Entertainment Enterprises Limited and others v zeebox Limited* [2014] EWCA Civ 82 and *The London Taxi Corporation Ltd (t/a as The London Taxi Company) v Frazer-Nash Research Ltd* [2015] EWHC 1840 (Ch)). Consequently, neither as witness recruitment programmes nor as surveys as such are surveys likely to feature significantly in future passing off cases. Parties will have to work out different ways to obtain evidence from individuals, which is likely to be difficult where a misrepresentation has only recently been made or only on a local scale.

If an action is brought before the defendant's launch, then pure advocacy and the judge's own assessment will form the major element of the case.

The individual defendant: joint tortfeasorship

Where a trader is a limited company but the company is essentially a one man vehicle, it is now becoming commonplace in the IPEC for the sole director of a companies to be found to be jointly liable passing off on the grounds that the director and his company were involved in a common design to carry out the acts passing their goods off as the claimants. The so-called corporate veil may offer no protection in such circumstances. In order to fix an alleged joint tortfeasor with liability, it must be shown both that they actively co-operated to bring about the act of the primary tortfeasor and also that they intended that their co-operation would help to bring about the act found to be tortious (*Vertical Leisure Ltd v Poleplus Ltd* [2015] EWHC 841 (IPEC)). In *Grenade (UK) Ltd v Grenade Energy Ltd* ([2016] EWHC 877 (IPEC)) the court held that registering a company name which itself reflected the claimant's brand and then allowing that name to be used in the course of trade made the director personally liable both for passing off and consequently the costs of fighting the claim. However, neither of these cases was reviewed by a higher court.

Remedies

The remedies available to a successful claimant include:

- a final injunction;
- either an inquiry as to damages or an account of profits, on the normal tortious basis;
- the less well-known options of an order for destruction or delivery up of offending items and/or tools for their manufacture; and
- publication of the judgment at the defendant's expense in a suitable channel such as trade press or online.

The latter remedy was introduced under the EU Enforcement of Intellectual Property Directive (2004/48/EC) and is surprisingly effective despite its limited cost: no one wishes to be ordered to tell the world at large that they have been found to be dishonest or even guilty of a misjudgment in any degree.

The measure of damages is the damages which naturally flow from the defendant's unlawful act (*Spalding v Gamage* (1918) 32 RPC 101), including any loss of trade but excluding speculative or unproven damage. The principal two heads are loss of sales, which could include loss of licensing revenue if the brand originator already licenses the brand, and damage to the goodwill of the business. Nominal damages will be awarded if the injunction (or simply bringing the claim) have led to the misrepresentation being discontinued before any actual damage has been suffered.

FURTHER READING

The Law of Passing-Off: Unfair Competition by Misrepresentation 4th ed, by Christopher Wadlow (2011) Sweet & Maxwell Ltd

Intellectual Property Law 5th ed. By Bently, Sherman, Ganjee and Johnson (2018) OUP

IPEC Guide:

https://assets.publishing.service.gov.uk/government/uploads/system/uploads/attachment_data/file/823201/intellectual-property-enterprise-guide.pdf

'A Practical Guide to Spousal Maintenance' by Liz Cowell
'A Practical Guide to the Law of Domain Names and Cybersquatting' by Andrew Clemson
'A Practical Guide to the Law of Gender Pay Gap Reporting' by Harini Iyengar
'A Practical Guide to the Rights of Grandparents in Children Proceedings' by Stuart Barlow
'NHS Whistleblowing and the Law' by Joseph England
'Employment Law and the Gig Economy' by Nigel Mackay & Annie Powell
'A Practical Guide to the General Data Protection Regulation (GDPR)' by Keith Markham
'A Practical Guide to Noise Induced Hearing Loss (NIHL) Claims' by Andrew Mckie, Ian Skeate, Gareth McAloon
'An Introduction to Beauty Negligence Claims – A Practical Guide for the Personal Injury Practitioner' by Greg Almond
'Intercompany Agreements for Transfer Pricing Compliance' by Paul Sutton
'Zen and the Art of Mediation' by Martin Plowman
'A Practical Guide to the SRA Principles, Individual and Law Firm Codes of Conduct 2019 – What Every Law Firm Needs to Know' by Paul Bennett
'A Practical Guide to Licensing Law for Commercial Property Lawyers' by Niall McCann & Richard Williams
'A Practical Guide to Adoption for Family Lawyers' by Graham Pegg
'A Practical Guide to Industrial Disease Claims' by Andrew Mckie & Ian Skeate
'A Practical Guide to Redundancy' by Philip Hyland
'A Practical Guide to Vicarious Liability' by Mariel Irvine
'A Practical Guide to Claims Arising from Delays in Diagnosing Cancer' by Bella Webb
'A Practical Guide to Applications for Landlord's Consent and Variation of Leases' by Mark Shelton
'A Practical Guide to Relief from Sanctions Post-Mitchell and Denton' by Peter Causton
'A Practical Guide to Equity Release for Advisors' by Paul Sams
'A Practical Guide to Unlawful Eviction and Harassment' by Stephanie Lovegrove

‘A Practical Guide to the Law Relating to Food’ by Ian Thomas
‘A Practical Guide to the Ending of Assured Shorthold Tenancies’ by Elizabeth Dwomoh
‘A Practical Guide to Financial Services Claims’ by Chris Hegarty
‘The Law of Houses in Multiple Occupation: A Practical Guide to HMO Proceedings’ by Julian Hunt
‘A Practical Guide to Unlawful Eviction and Harassment’ by Stephanie Lovegrove
‘A Practical Guide to Solicitor and Client Costs’ by Robin Dunne
‘A Practical Guide to Wrongful Conception, Wrongful Birth and Wrongful Life Claims’ by Rebecca Greenstreet
‘Occupiers, Highways and Defective Premises Claims: A Practical Guide Post-Jackson – 2nd Edition’ by Andrew Mckie
‘A Practical Guide to Financial Ombudsman Service Claims’ by Adam Temple & Robert Scrivenor
‘A Practical Guide to the Law of Enfranchisement and Lease Extension’ by Paul Sams
‘A Practical Guide to Marketing for Lawyers – 2nd Edition’ by Catherine Bailey & Jennet Ingram
'A Practical Guide to Advising Schools on Employment Law' by Jonathan Holden
'Certificates of Lawful Use and Development: A Guide to Making and Determining Applications' by Bob Mc Geady & Meyric Lewis
‘A Guide to Consent in Clinical Negligence Post-Montgomery’ by Lauren Sutherland QC
‘A Practical Guide to Running Housing Disrepair and Cavity Wall Claims: 2nd Edition’ by Andrew Mckie & Ian Skeate
‘A Practical Guide to Holiday Sickness Claims – 2nd Edition’ by Andrew Mckie & Ian Skeate
‘Arguments and Tactics for Personal Injury and Clinical Negligence Claims’ by Dorian Williams
‘A Practical Guide to QOCS and Fundamental Dishonesty’ by James Bentley
‘A Practical Guide to Drone Law’ by Rufus Ballaster, Andrew Firman, Eleanor Clot
‘A Practical Guide to Compliance for Personal Injury Firms Working With Claims Management Companies’ by Paul Bennett

'A Practical Guide to the Landlord and Tenant Act 1954: Commercial Tenancies' by Richard Hayes & David Sawtell
'A Practical Guide to Dog Law for Owners and Others' by Andrea Pitt
'RTA Allegations of Fraud in a Post-Jackson Era: The Handbook – 2nd Edition' by Andrew Mckie
'RTA Personal Injury Claims: A Practical Guide Post-Jackson' by Andrew Mckie
'On Experts: CPR35 for Lawyers and Experts' by David Boyle
'An Introduction to Personal Injury Law' by David Boyle
'A Practical Guide to Claims Arising From Accidents Abroad and Travel Claims' by Andrew Mckie & Ian Skeate
'A Practical Guide to Chronic Pain Claims' by Pankaj Madan
'A Practical Guide to Claims Arising from Fatal Accidents' by James Patience
'A Practical Approach to Clinical Negligence Post-Jackson' by Geoffrey Simpson-Scott
'Employers' Liability Claims: A Practical Guide Post-Jackson' by Andrew Mckie
'A Practical Guide to Subtle Brain Injury Claims' by Pankaj Madan
'A Practical Guide to Costs in Personal Injury Cases' by Matthew Hoe
'The No Nonsense Solicitors' Practice: A Guide To Running Your Firm' by Bettina Brueggemann
'The Queen's Counsel Lawyer's Omnibus: 20 Years of Cartoons from The Times 1993-2013' by Alex Steuart Williams

These books and more are available to order online direct from the publisher at www.lawbriefpublishing.com, where you can also read free sample chapters. For any queries, contact us on 0844 587 2383 or mail@lawbriefpublishing.com.

Our books are also usually in stock at www.amazon.co.uk with free next day delivery for Prime members, and at good legal bookshops such as Wildy & Sons.

We are regularly launching new books in our series of practical day-to-day practitioners' guides. Visit our website and join our free newsletter to be kept informed and to receive special offers, free chapters, etc.

You can also follow us on Twitter at www.twitter.com/lawbriefpub.

www.ingramcontent.com/pod-product-compliance
Lightning Source LLC
Chambersburg PA
CBHW051151180926
51611CB00001B/25
* 9 7 8 1 9 1 2 6 8 7 7 7 0 *